# COACH TO COACH

Business Lessons from
the Locker Room

John Robinson

**Pfeiffer**
**& COMPANY**

Johannesburg • Oxford
San Diego • Sydney • Toronto

This publication is designed to provide accurate and authoritative information in regard to the subject matter covered. It is sold with the understanding that the publisher is not engaged in rendering legal, accounting, or other professional service. If legal advice or other expert assistance is required, the services of a competent professional person should be sought. *From a Declaration of Principles jointly adopted by a Committee of the American Bar Association and a Committee of Publishers.*

Cover Design: Paul Bond
Cover Illustration: Kathleen Blavatt
Interior Design: Lee Ann Hubbard
Page Composition: Norine Neely
Editor: JoAnn Padgett
Production Editor: Dawn Kilgore
Editorial Assistant: Susan Rachmeler

Published by Pfeiffer & Company
8517 Production Avenue
San Diego, CA 92121-2280
United States of America

Editorial Offices:
(619) 578-5900, FAX (619) 578-2042
Orders:
USA (606) 647-3030, FAX (606) 647-3034
ISBN: 0-89384-274-5

Printed in the United States of America.

Printing 1 2 3 4 5 6 7 8 9 10

**Library of Congress Cataloging-in-Publication Data**

Robinson, John, 1935—
    Coach to coach: business lessons from the locker room / John Robinson.
        p.   cm. — (Warren Bennis executive briefing series)
    Includes index.
    ISBN 0-89384-274-5
    1. Football—Coaching—Philosophy.   2. Teamwork (Sports)
3. Leadership.   I. Title.   II. Series.
GV954.4.R63   1996                         95-40337
796.332'07'7—dc20                            CIP

# Dedication

*To all the players*
*I have ever had the privilege to coach.*

# Contents

# Acknowledgments

This book was not my idea. The fact that it is now seeing the light of day is a tribute in great part to others, especially:

Warren Bennis, whose vision for it was convincing and whose confidence led me to do it.

Anne Coyle, who helped me get the words right on paper.

JoAnn Padgett, whose willingness to work with my schedule and whose supportiveness during the various drafts helped to make it a better book.

My wife Linda, who supported this effort uncomplainingly, despite the fact that it ate into the little free time my coaching life allows.

The team of people who supported all of us.

And last, Karla Swatek, whose work begins now that all's said and done.

To all, I want to say "thank you."

# Editor's Preface

Teamwork, the essence of football, is fast becoming the norm in business. As organizations shift toward team-based work, management must focus on coaching skills and the increased empowerment of workers.

Football teams turn over personnel every season. Their aggressive recruiting methods combined with their ability to rapidly meld diverse individuals into a cohesive unit and inspire intense team loyalty provide an excellent model for today's business teams. Corporate teams are often "virtual" teams, task forces, or cross-functional teams that, like the football team, must quickly unite various individual abilities, attitudes, and skills into a powerful, effective force.

A football team's flexibility and horizontal movement of players is the direction that today's business teams are headed. The conventional approach of business has been to recruit individuals to fill a functional rather than an organizational objective. One does not necessarily follow the other, and learning organizations are discovering the value of recruiting for the big picture, for the organization's needs. The reality is that organizational health is dependent upon successful team action. Football coaches have always recognized this truth.

In *Coach to Coach*, John Robinson views coaching through a wide-angle lens. He does not limit his perspective to a process with a set number of steps; he knows that coaching is more fluid and dynamic than that. In explaining the work that he loves, Coach Robinson examines the prerequisites to a successful coaching effort, key elements of the coaching craft, the relationships among and responsibilities of the total team—the leader, assistant coaches, players—and the ongoing commitment to continuous improvement.

Coach Robinson, considered by many to be football's top collegiate recruiter, recognizes that you cannot coach success unless you recruit talent first. He coaches you to do both. He examines why this seemingly obvious truth is so often overlooked by organizations, and he discusses the consequences of this behavior.

Another dimension of a coach's leadership is his vision and values. If an organization wants its employees to work productively as a team, there must be a clear vision and there must be unanimity around that vision. There must be consistent policies and procedures to give the vision credibility.

Attitude, knowledge, talent, and vision all affect how people do their jobs. Coach Robinson examines how to approach business, sports, or any significant endeavor with vision, enthusiasm, and a passion to be the best. John Robinson is a friend and colleague. He represents USC with pride and dignity and displays an honest love and passion for what he does. He loves his job and, as a result, he does it well.

A coach has a unique job. Unlike most other positions where an individual seeks to gain recognition through personal achievement and accomplishment, the coach's success is based on an ability to inspire others to high performance and success. Whether in football or in business, the goal is to get the most, the best performance, out of people. Their success is the coach's reward. *Coach to Coach* can help you and your organization realize this reward.

*Warren Bennis*
*Santa Monica, California*

# Author's Preface

Although I can imagine, in the not-to-distant future, more coed athletic teams in school and professional sports, my experience in coaching collegiate and professional football has been with the male of the species. I know many talented people of both genders. However, I find the use of s/he constructions or the alternating use of "he" and "she" to be distracting to the reader. Thus, I beg your tolerance of the use of the pronoun "he" throughout this book. The information I have to share in this book pertains equally to men and women.

*John Robinson*
*Pasadena, California*

# Foreword

What John Robinson has to say in this book makes a lot of sense because he has been talking about the same things all of his life—sports and coaching—being the best, working the hardest, and winning.

We grew up together in Daly City, California, and always talked and dreamed about doing two things in our lives—playing football as long as we could...then coaching. John did that and did it as one of the best.

Throughout our careers, we've spent hours on the phone and days together talking about football and our jobs. At first, the conversations were just centered around football—plays, pass coverage, fundamentals, and strategies. When we became head coaches, the subjects changed—leadership, management, organization, motivation, teamwork—"the tough stuff"!! That is what we talked about and that is what this book is about.

John is a friend for life—intelligent, funny, insightful, strategic—what the heck more do you need than that?

*John Madden*

# COACHES AND COACHING

# Introduction

*The coach is the coach, parent, friend, lawyer, role model and*
*everything rolled into one.*

*USA Today*

I grew up with John Madden [former NFL Raiders'
coach and now a sports commentator]. I remember
when we were fifteen or sixteen, sitting together on a
bench in Marchbank Park in Daly City, California. It was
1953. We were dreaming-talking about how we were
both going into coaching, and how if one guy got ahead
faster, he would hire the other.

Fast-forward to 1977. I was standing outside the
Raiders' locker room after they had won Super Bowl XI,
where one week prior we had won the Rose Bowl. At the
time, I was the head coach at USC [the University of
Southern California]. John, of course was the coach of

1

*In the 1977 Rose Bowl, it was USC 14, Michigan 6.*

the winning Raiders. When John came out of the locker room, we just looked at each other and laughed. There we were, two clowns who twenty years prior were sitting, dreaming that we would be great coaches. And it happened! I am struck with how dreams have such a powerful influence on one's life. Not only did it come true for us, but we also had that powerful coincidence of both winning the highest honors in our respective areas in the same stadium and within one week of each other.

How did it happen? Was it mere chance? What were the elements that influenced it? I believe that adolescent dream shaped my life. And, as I look back, it is clear that many people supported my pursuit of that vision. These people were teachers and mentors to me. They influenced me and challenged me; they caught my imagination and encouraged me.

*John Madden celebrates his team's 1977 Super Bowl XI victory over the Minnesota Vikings at Pasadena's Rose Bowl.*

## MENTORS AND MODELS

Five men in my life had a profound influence on me—all of them coaches. Each helped me develop in significant ways. They helped shape and nurture my early ambition. I am indebted to each of them for facets of what I believe today about coaching. These people all made demands of me; they had expectations of me that I could not have conceived of at the time. I was no Joe Montana who was going to reflect shared greatness on them. Yet, they cared about me, not just as a player, but as a young man and as a human being who shared their enthusiasm for a game I love. Nowadays, as I talk to coaches, many of the coaching philosophies I share with them are a product of those early influences and of my own enthusiasm to learn.

## GLEN SMITH

My first great coaching influence was Glen Smith, the summer recreation director in Marchbank Park. Of all the things I learned from him, probably the most important was how to try hard. He challenged us, drove us, and cajoled us into trying much harder than any of us knew that we could. He forced us to compete beyond our level, then he rewarded us for trying. In the process, we learned to love the experience.

*In those days, your head coach was God. You showed him respect; like you did your parents.*[1]

Three of my friends—John Madden, Ray Rosa, Dan Bartelli—and I went to that park every day for several summers, from the ages of eleven through around fifteen. We learned a lot about growing up from Glen Smith. Absolute starvation was the only thing that made us go home. Every day we would grab breakfast and arrive at the park by 8:00 a.m. Usually we scraped together enough money to buy lunch so that we did not have to leave. We would not go home until at least 6:00 p.m., and sometimes we returned after dinner to play more. All summer long, that was our life. Glen Smith influenced us because he taught us how to try our hardest, how to compete, and how to survive in a group. He demanded that we grow up.

Smith was a big guy—about two hundred and fifty pounds. He ran that park like an absolute ruler. The only organization was what he decided. If he said, "We're playing football today," that is what we did. It could just as easily have been baseball, dodgeball, or wrestling.

*If you stood up and were a competitor, he paid attention to and included you. As long as you tried, you passed his test.*

Some days he would produce boxing gloves. Everyone had to fight. If someone said, "I don't want to play," they were banished! And if someone was a "baby" one day, he had to regain the right to play the next day. This guy was very demanding—all in the name of play. And while there were times we hated it, we also loved it.

As I look back on it, the guy was kind of a genius in the way he could keep different age groups playing together and learning. When there was a game, he made everybody play. You might have been twelve, but you were in a game with seventeen-year-olds. And these were big guys—seniors in high school, stars of the high school football team. We were in awe of them, so we were forced to prove ourselves when we played touch football. We would get knocked around.

I can remember each of us pouting at some time because someone had treated us badly. If we reacted that way, we were teased tremendously. When we got into wrestling matches with some bigger guys, we had to stand up for ourselves. It was not so much that there were knock-down-drag-out fights. The issue was having to prove ourselves. If someone was a sissy, he could not play. So we learned to make sure that no one thought we were sissies. We learned how to earn the older guys' respect.

Smith had a great sense of fair play. While he challenged the younger kids, he did not let the older guys get out of line either. And he had a great reward system. If you were afraid or lazy, he would get down on you. If you stood up and were a competitor, he paid attention to and included you. As long as you tried, you passed his test. We learned and became worthy of that attention.

## JESS FREITAS

My high school coach, Jess Freitas, also had a great influence on me, in a different way. He was a stern and not particularly verbal guy. He seldom complimented us, and when he did it might be just a nod. Like Glen Smith, he demanded that we prove ourselves deserving.

He was a great student of the game. I thought he knew everything, that he was the smartest football coach who ever lived. He was the ultimate authority when it came to football. He taught us how to play the game very well. We won games we should have lost; the other teams were better. Our advantage was that we were smarter, or at least we always thought we were. We knew how to play the game better because he had taught us. He called great plays. Coach Freitas taught us a great respect for the game and the discipline of the game. I was successful as a player there.

## LEN CASANOVA

After high school I was fortunate enough to get a scholarship to the University of Oregon. Len Casanova was the head coach at Oregon at the time. Casanova is in the College Football Hall of Fame. In addition to being a great coach, he was a great human being. You always knew Cas—everyone called him Cas—cared about you. I was not a very good player in college. I was not a star, but he never treated me differently than anybody else. He just demanded your top performance. If you did not perform,

*I was not a very good player in college. I was not a star, but he never treated me differently than anybody else.*

UPI/Bettmann

*Keeping their chins and hearts high in defeat, Oregon players "chair" their coach Len Casanova from the field after losing the 1958 Rose Bowl to Ohio State by the slim margin of 7-10.*

University of Oregon Archives, Eugene, Oregon

*Len Casnova's 1958 University of Oregon coaching staff included two future NFL coaches—George Seifert, 2nd from left (San Francisco 49ers) and John Robinson, 3rd from right*

**At the University of Oregon, Len Casanova led Oregon to three post-season bowl appearances; the 1958 Rose Bowl, the 1960 Liberty Bowl, and the 1963 Sun Bowl. During his 21-year collegiate head coaching career (begun at Santa Clara in 1946), he accumulated a mark of 104-97-10. He began his final season (1966) as the 14th winningest active head coach in the country. 2**

he would get on you something fierce. It was humiliating, but I never remember being angry at him for that. It was bad when you screwed up, and Cas was not one of those guys who said it was okay. But you also knew that you mattered to him.

My own father died when I was a freshman; he had been sick for a couple of years. In some ways Cas became a father figure to me. I remember one incident in particular with certain gratitude toward the man. During training camp, I cracked some ribs. I kept practicing, even though I was in a lot of pain, but it started to get to me. I started to rationalize that maybe I was not cut out for this and that I should leave the university and do something else with my life. I talked to Cas about the idea. Cas had a great intuitive knowledge of human nature. He was willing to listen. He probably said to himself, "This guy is wimping out. If I give him a break, maybe he'll suck his courage back up." Of course that is not what he said. He just looked at me and said, "That's not what you want to do." Then he had me go to his house instead of football practice. He had a swimming pool; I'd never been in a house with a swimming pool! His wife brought me Cokes while I just lay around. That evening, when I went back to training camp for dinner, my dilemma was over. Cas never brought it up again.

Cas's very strong moral influence meant a lot to everybody. He was a devout Catholic, and because I was Catholic too, he would check on me on Sundays. Years later when he would call, my first reaction was to think, "Did I go to church? Is he going to be on my case again?"

Living up to his standards was ingrained in us. If you could just live by the standards he embodied, everything would be okay.

From Cas I learned a lot about the human side of coaching—the importance of example, of listening to players, of giving straight feedback, and the role of caring for the whole person, not just the set of talents that a player brings to his team.

## JOHN MCKAY

*USC Sports Information*

*John McKay was inducted into the College Football Hall of Fame in 1988.*

While I was at Oregon, there was an assistant coach there named John McKay. John may have had the most significant influence on me. I knew I wanted to be like him. McKay knew football. He is the smartest coach I have ever known. I used to go to his office in the off-season to see if he would teach me about the game. He was always willing to spend time with me. When I think of it now, it was like a rocket scientist teaching a high school kid math. He taught me how to think about football, how much there was to learn, and how to learn about it. He taught me that you have to think about it constantly, to be on your mind all the time, that to be any good at this game you have to be totally committed to it.

After Oregon, McKay went on to tremendous success as head coach at USC. I will always remember an incident when John Madden was an assistant coach at a junior college and I was a freshman coach at Oregon. McKay, who had just won the national championship and been named 1962 National Coach of the Year, was giving a clinic that John and I attended—along with 2,000 other people. After McKay finished, we stayed around to say hello and wave at him. McKay was surrounded by a lot people talking to him. Turning around, he saw John and me and yelled, "Hey, you two guys.

John McKay was USC's head coach from 1960-1975 and accumulated a mark of 127-40-8, including two national titles (1972, 1974) and three bowl victories. [3]

UPI/Bettmann

*John Madden and star quarter-back Kenny Stabler*

Stand right there!" If he had not remembered to come over to us when he was through, we would probably still be standing there! After everybody left, he took us out for a drink and we talked football for about two hours. There we were, two nobodies, but he knew we liked football. McKay liked people who liked football.

Ten years later, he hired me at USC. I learned a lot from him about how to create successful strategies and about how to coach individuals to develop winning teamwork.

## JOHN MADDEN

John Madden also had a big influence on my career. We were peers. We stimulated each other. Throughout our youth, we would talk football and argue. If one of us said 2 + 2 = 4, the other guy was not necessarily going to agree to that. As I said before, we had agreed that the first one of us who became a head coach would hire the other. John progressed fast. At 32, Al Davis hired John as the head coach of the Raiders. When that happened, John called me to ask if I wanted a job, but it was not the right time for me to leave Oregon. Years later I did go to Oakland to work for John for a year. That was a great year. We had a lot of fun together and it really cemented our friendship. He was the boss. He treated me great. And we had a very good team.

**John Madden coached the Raiders from 1969-1978 and led the team to 7 division championships, an AFC championship, and a 1977 Super Bowl XI World Championship.[4]**

John has a great ability to handle different types of people. He can separate what is important from what is not. He demands a lot in important areas, but he could care less about insignificant things. The players' appearances or lifestyles did not matter. All that mattered was that they knew how to give their best. John took people from a variety of lifestyles and backgrounds and built them into a team with a common purpose. He knew how to give people space, yet be very demanding when it mattered. His team performed and was very loyal.

## THE LEGACY

*If you are going to be a role model or a leader, you have to learn how to coach.*

Those are the men who made the biggest difference in my personal development. I am sure there are people like that who have made a difference in yours. In most lives, the teacher-coach plays a very important role. While coaching might not be your career, most of us perform a coaching role at some time in our lives: as a parent, businessperson, or community leader. If you are going to be a role model or a leader, you have to learn how to coach. Coaching, and the ability to coach, is important for everyone. And it can become one of the most enjoyable experiences in your life!

To me, coaching is a real calling. It is my career; it is what I do. And I think it is the greatest job out there. We have the opportunity, the challenge, the privilege...really, of helping people build on their strengths, develop their enjoyment, and accomplish dreams. Doing that is rewarding. To do that, we cannot succeed unless we are willing to deal with the whole person and not just the particular skills that we are coaching. We are teachers certainly, but we are much more than that. A coach plays many roles: at times teacher, parent, motivator, friend, role model, and task master.

How I think about coaching today is a result of people's influences and key experiences along the way. In the following chapters, I would like to share some of those thoughts with you. It is really quite simple and comes down to:

- Seeing it before you do it—you have to have vision.

- Loving what you do, the process you are involved in—not just the end result.

- Building the team and building teamwork.

# John Robinson's Head Coaching Record

## USC

| YEAR | W | L | T | PAC-10 FINISH | BOWL | RANKING |
|------|---|---|---|------|------|---------|
| 1976* | 11 | 1 | 0 | 1st | Rose win | 2nd in AP, UPI |
| 1977 | 8 | 4 | 0 | 2nd | Bluebonnet win | 12th tie in UPI 13th in AP |
| 1978** | 12 | 1 | 0 | 1st | Rose win | 1st in UPI 2nd in AP |
| 1979*** | 11 | 0 | 1 | 1st | Rose win | 2nd in AP, UPI |
| 1980 | 8 | 2 | 1 | 3rd | | 11th in AP 12th in UPI |
| 1981 | 9 | 3 | 0 | 2nd | Fiesta loss | 13th in UPI 14th in AP |
| 1982 | 8 | 3 | 0 | 3rd | | 14th in USA Today/CNN 15th in AP |
| 1993 | 8 | 5 | 0 | 1st (tie) | Freedom win | 25th in USA Today/CNN, UPI |
| 1994 | 8 | 3 | 1 | 2nd (tie) | Cotton win | 13th in AP, UPI, 15th in USA Today/CNN |
| TOTAL | 83 | 22 | 3 | .782 | (9 years) | |

*PAC-8 and West Coast Coach of the Year
**PAC-10 and West Coast Coach of the Year
***National Coach of the Year

## Los Angeles Rams

| YEAR | W | L | NFC WEST FINISH | PLAYOFFS |
|------|---|---|------|----------|
| 1983 | 9 | 7 | 2nd | Lost in first-round playoff game |
| 1984 | 10 | 6 | 2nd | Lost in wild-card playoff game |
| 1985 | 11 | 5 | 1st | Lost in NFC championship game |
| 1986 | 10 | 6 | 2nd | Lost in first-round playoff game |
| 1987 | 6 | 9 | 3rd | Did not make playoffs |
| 1988 | 10 | 6 | 2nd | Lost in first-round playoff game |
| 1989 | 11 | 5 | 2nd | Lost in NFC championship game |
| 1990 | 5 | 11 | 3rd | Did not make playoffs |
| 1991 | 3 | 13 | 4th | Did not make playoffs |
| Playoffs | 4 | 6 | | |
| TOTAL (9 yrs.) | 79 | 74 | | .516 |
| CAREER (18 yrs.) | 162 | 96 | 3rd | .626 |

*USC Sports Information*

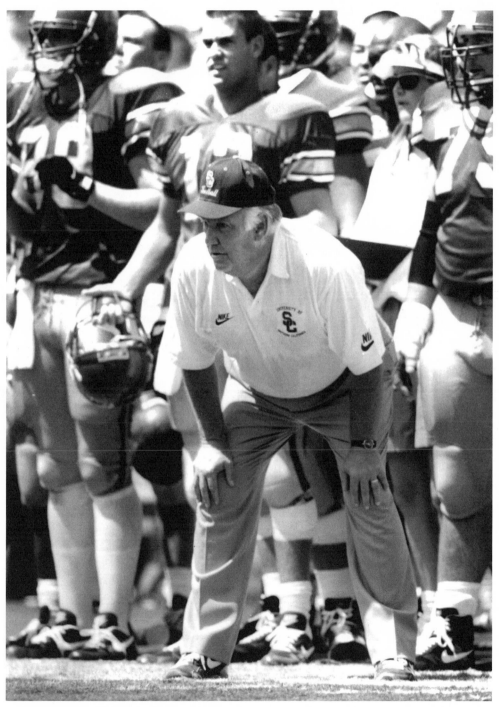

*USC Sports Information*

# PART ONE

*If* you want to do something significant, you must be able to dream about it, to project yourself into the achievement, and to see what matters about it. Walt Disney used to say, "If you can dream it, you can do it." I would go even further and say, "What you dream is what you become."

# SEE IT
# BEFORE YOU DO IT

**1**

*Like an internal magnet, yearnings pull us toward one thing
instead of another, a process that begins in early
childhood.... Often those early yearnings are so powerful they
chart the course of one's lifework.*

Donald O. Clifton and Paula Nelson,
*Soar With Your Strengths*

## ANYONE CAN DO IT

Everyone fantasizes about their future. While the vision
is often sketchy about how it will be accomplished, it is
always rich in how it will feel. Children do this all the
time. They constantly project themselves
into different characters. They watch
characters or sports personalities in the
media, then they mimic their heroes'
characteristics and style. As a kid, I practiced the batting stances of baseball players I had seen on television. I pretended
I was them. I did not hit very well, but I
had a lot of great stances.

*There is no doubt that such
dreams influence who we become.
They become the due north on
our compass.*

It is natural for children and young adults to fantasize and dream about their future. What happens to this as we grow up? When do we stop dreaming? It seems that the closer we get to realizing a dream, the less ability we have to project ourselves into it. Increasing our ability to "see" the future, to envision it, is crucial to every success.

There are three types of vision:

1. Life vision, which John Madden and I shared,

2. Make-something-happen vision, which provides a road map for the team or company, and

3. Rehearsal vision, which helps us achieve events every day.

All of these visions have texture and emotion. They are like short film clips or a series of freeze-frames. Each type has a role in building success.

## LIFE VISION

As children, we try out different self-images to answer the question "What do I want to be when I grow up?" As teenagers, that image becomes more attuned to reality. We discover things done by people that we admire, that we enjoy doing, or that we are good at. We decide to become a pilot or a painter or a piano player. We can see and feel what it is like to fly a plane, paint a picture, or play at a concert. We project ourselves into these fantasies. There is no doubt that such dreams influence who we become. They become the due north on our compass. They are the stimuli that focus our attention on all kinds of experiences: people, books, shows, or the subjects that we study.

It is important to be able to share a life vision with your best friend, your mate, your colleague, your mentor, your boss. Thinking back on my life, it was my good fortune to have a great friend, John, whose life vision paralleled mine. This shared focus allowed us to articulate our dreams and enhance them.

> *T*o continue dreaming is to continue growing.

Adults in the pursuit of careers often let their life vision fizzle out. They think they have arrived at their destination, and they become absorbed with the what's happening in the present.

Once we are into the nuts and bolts of our careers, we often forget to think of the future or to project ourselves into the next job, to see ourselves as the president, or further up the chain of command. The same thing happens in other aspects of our lives—our families, our relationships.

When we are younger and thinking about our futures, we are hopeful and expectant. We should keep that hopefulness forever.

> *We should not let ourselves become passive victims of whatever current we happen to be sailing in.*

As we get older, there are so many things to dream about—the character and values we want to project; our dreams for our marriage, family, career; the experiences we want to have or that we want our children to have; the countries or cultures we want to experience first-hand; the boat or plane we want to buy or the house we want to build.

There are always new adventures if we only stop to imagine them. The broader our horizons, the more rich and varied our lives become. This life vision keeps us looking ahead. It gives us a window on what the future can be. Keeping this ability alive keeps you sailing ahead. To me, this is the real value of maintaining our ability to dream.

# MAKE-SOMETHING-HAPPEN VISION

*USC Sports Information*

*Lynn Swann, 1973 USC Team Co-Captain, went on to a successful career as wide receiver for the Pittsburgh Steelers (1974-1982).*

**The 1978 team may have been the most talented in college football history. Thirty-five players from it went on to the NFL, including two Heisman Trophy winners—Charles White and Marcus Allen (not to mention Anthony Muñoz, Ronnie Lott, Dennis Smith, Clay Matthews and Dennis Thurman).[1]**

The closer we get to realizing a life vision, the more specific our vision has to be. It becomes a different kind of vision. It is now a more predictable future event, so we focus more finely. Past experiences help us fill in the outlines and give us approaches and details. This make-something-happen vision is a more strategic vision. It defines the way you would like your life, your organization, or your team to be. It starts in your own mind but must be shared by everyone involved. If it is not clear to you, if it is not something that you care about, if it is not visual and creative, there is a good chance that you will not communicate it well and that you will lose track of where you are going once you try to make it happen. If it is vividly conceived in your mind, then you have a good chance of making it happen. The vision comes first; the plan to support it comes out of that.

When I returned to USC, it was crucial that I have a vision for what USC football was going to be in the 1990s. That vision had to be active and pertinent to the current situation. Of course I wanted us to be winners again. There had been a clear vision of USC football in the 70s. It was one of the great decades of Trojan [USC mascot] history. Coming back, it was seductive to want to re-create that vision. And there are parts that we are re-creating. But ours must be a vision that can be successful now—a vision to guide us in understanding who we are, what we stand for, how we look, how we act, and what it feels like to be part of our team.

What it took to be successful in college football in the 1980s is very different from what it takes to be successful in the 1990s. My absence made it easier to see just how much. Opponents had changed—other universities had caught up. Rule changes made it more difficult for USC to win. Both facts required that we do things differently. People who had been at USC all along doing the same job but getting different results may have felt confused and disillusioned. The first step toward implementing a new vision was for everyone to be able to admit, "We've got to do it better."

An organization can fail if its vision becomes stagnant. A vision has to evolve constantly. Even if a vision embodies the fundamentals, you should be aware that fundamentals change, granted, sometimes as slowly and imperceptibly as a glacier moves. Whenever I watch a NASA launch and see the towers that launch the rocket slowly move into place, I think that here is the essence of their work. That slow, incredibly careful movement is how I see us moving our vision into place. And it, too, is our launch pad. The leader is responsible for continual evaluation of the vision and forward movement. People sometimes resist a new vision for the organization. If your people bought into your original vision, they are going to resist changes. There is security in staying the same. Established organizations that become uncompetitive are often guilty of this.

At times I hear people tell me "Back in the old days we did it this way." "Back in the 70s we did it this way. And it was good!" I have to remind myself that this person would never look at his own business and say, "This is the way we did it in the 70s and we're going to do it the same way now." We have to see the need to change and be able to stick to the hard course that our new vision demands. Building a new reality presents lots of opportunities to get bogged down, but a vision must be fluid and constantly revisited so that it never stagnates.

For us to get back on top, we needed to make some real changes—in personnel, in

*USC Sports Information*

*Pat Haden, USC Quarterback and 1974 Team Co-Captain, who went on to quarterback the Los Angeles Rams from 1976-1981.*

### USC 18, Ohio State 17
### 1975 Rose Bowl

Rhodes scholar Pat Haden threw a 38-yard touchdown pass late in the game to John McKay, the coach's son, then fired a 2-point conversion pass to Shelton Diggs to give USC a narrow 18-17 win over Ohio State and the national title. Haden threw for 181 yards and 2 touchdowns to offset the loss of Anthony Davis, who suffered a rib injury.[2]

USC Sports Information

*Charles White, USC's third Heisman Trophy winner (1979), finished his four-year career as the NCAA's second leading rusher ever with 5,598 regular season yards.*

### USC 17, Ohio State 16 1980 Rose Bowl

USC's Heisman Trophy winning tailback Charles White stole the show as he led the Trojans to a come-from-behind win in one of the most exciting games in Rose Bowl history. White, named Player of the Game for the second straight year, rushed for a Rose Bowl record 247 yards, including a 1-yard touchdown dive with 1:32 remaining in the game that gave USC the win.[3]

coaching, and in capital. To actually become national champions, we have to constantly reestablish our expectations, resell our school, and realize that we must do better. The coaches have to coach better. The players have to play better. We must wrestle with how we are to do that.

Once a program has slipped it takes a tremendous effort to bring it back. It is easy to lose momentum. You cannot back off of your effort. I am sure it is the same in any business. People get tired. They start to say, "Things are okay. We're doing fine" or "Business is good. Sales are up" or "We're making progress." But you may be losing ground on your future. That is the hardest thing to see. You have to constantly remind yourself of what is needed and of what needs to happen. Let your vision help you take stock. Talk about what you see. Encourage people for what they have achieved. But continue to highlight the image you are shooting for.

An organization needs to constantly upgrade itself. The marketplace and competition keep changing. Technology keeps changing. A leader must constantly reevaluate what it takes to win. What it took to win last year will not necessarily win this year. Unfortunately, success can breed a kind of complacency or arrogance that results in a shrinking percentage of growth from year to year. An attitude of "if it ain't broke, don't fix it" condemns you to finding out that you let it break. So each year you need to adjust the vision, the effort, and the performance from the year before. It is easier to talk about what you did to win in the past than to look at the challenges facing you. And the last time around you were probably *doing it*, not just sitting around talking about it! Focus on the future, not the past. When you have been successful, it takes a lot of courage to say, "We'll come up with something new," This is what innovative business leaders refer to when they talk about "raising the bar."

## CHECK YOUR PLANS
## AGAINST THE VISION

I can see us in the Rose Bowl—what the bus ride , that game, and the press conference will be like. I can see us as the national champions. Those images come spontaneously. I almost cannot stop them. These are not images that come when you are trying to convince yourself of something; they are involuntary projections of the potential I know is there. Out of these images comes certainty about how to prepare. These images guide my planning.

*USC Sports Information*

*Marcus Allen, USC's fourth Heisman Trophy winner (1981), was college football's first 2,000-yard rusher. He went on to play as a running back for the Los Angeles Raiders (1982-1992) and for the Kansas City Chiefs (1993-1994).*

If I try to plan cold, nothing happens. But driving home, seven things may visually pop into my head. Once the vision is there, I can begin to translate it into plans. At those times, ideas flow and build, the connections pop.

When I am implementing the vision—in execution mode—I am planning, analyzing, doing. This is a different way of thinking about the team. I am in the middle of it. To visualize, I have to step back from the job. The big picture is much more vivid when I am driving, on a plane, or on vacation than it is when I am actually on the job. During the season, we are on the job twelve and fourteen hours a day. Then it is hard to distance myself, to just sit and think about what we are doing, to check the plans against the vision, to get perspective.

For me to be successful, I have to find perspective in little spaces of time during the week. Everything becomes clear to me when I take the time to visualize Saturday's game—who is going to win and what is going to happen. When the game finally arrives, it is as if I have already been there. I am at my best if I can do this. If not, I get more nervous and jittery the closer the game gets. In those instances, I know that I affect others negatively, just as I know that I affect others positively when I have a rehearsal vision of what is going to happen. Dennis Harrah, a great offensive lineman with the Rams, once told me, "I can tell on Tuesdays or Wednesdays how our team is going to do just by looking at you. The look in your eye, the sound of your voice, and the energy that comes off of you affects everybody." He startled me when he said that. But that is the difference in being able to balance vision with execution .

Getting a little distance now and then refreshes our vision. People need sabbaticals or time-outs. It allows them to step back and get perspective on their lives. None of us have much spare time. Whether thirty seconds or three minutes, breaks are important in helping us take stock of ourselves, to compare "now" and "then" photographs, as it were. If we become overwhelmed by the pressures and the responsibilities of our jobs, it helps to find brief moments when we can put everything in perspective.

After I left the Rams I spent a year out of football, with a lot of time on my hands. It was like a sabbatical. I was completely regenerated by that experience. It gave me an almost totally new resolve about my life. It was clear to me as I looked back that I had been "burning out" toward the end of my tenure. I had become engrossed in solving problems and neglected pulling away to get perspective on the larger picture. Had I been more reflective, I might have been able to change our downward cycle.

## A Shared Vision

No leader can achieve a vision alone. It has to be shared by the coaching staff and the team. It has to become our vision. The vision should not be so tightly sketched that no one else can contribute to it.

*Make sure your partners get to shape the vision you are working toward.*

Sharing a vision means giving your partners an opportunity to add details and modifications that mark their ownership. You must talk about it as "our" vision.

People may claim that they have so much faith in you that they accept your vision in totality. Don't believe it. Such people are the first ones to leave when the going gets tough—as it inevitably will. They are less committed because they do not own the vision. It is yours alone—not theirs and yours. Make sure your partners get to shape the vision you are working toward.

People will not embrace your vision unless it builds on what they care about. This is the key challenge when making a major change. Whenever someone assumes a position of leadership in an organization, he must acknowledge the existing culture and tradition. I was fortunate to have been identified with the past great USC tradition. But many new leaders, coaches, and players who come into an organization are regarded as outsiders. It is a serious mistake to think that they are going to change everything, and they jeopardize their chance for success.

If a team is in total and utter chaos or has no tradition, then starting over becomes your only option. Where there is an ongoing culture, that culture *must* be appreciated. It reflects this group's identity. That culture may have failed to a degree, but it can still have a lot of good in it. There may have been a temporary faltering in the organization, but not everything failed. If the organization built an ethic and had past successes but is going through a rough time, it needs help to fix the percentage that is not working.

The new leader must take traditions into account and build on them. He must bring a new ethic and simultaneously embrace the old one. The trick is to make people think that the new is just part of the old.

## COMMUNICATING THE VISION

Communicating a vision takes a lot of creativity. We may struggle to articulate a vivid mental image when our actions can communicate our vision as well as or better than our words. If my vision includes promptness, but I am twenty minutes late, it is not going to "take."

> *Words are meaningless when actions contradict them; actions have to be consistent with words.*

My friend Joe Rothman was a top manager with the Marriott Corporation. Joe was fabulous with people, one of the best. He communicated the image and vision of his hotel in such a way that everybody who worked there shared his vision of what the hotel should be like.

What starts with vision works down to practical things: the appearance of employees, the look on their faces, how they say hello, the hotel's appearance. You can bet that almost every employee walking down a hall in Joe's hotel, upon seeing a piece of litter on the floor, would bend down and pick it up. Joe would pick it up. His secretary would pick it up. Valets would pick it up. They would feel guilty for not picking it up because litter does not fit their vision and image of the company. There are lots of places where that litter would stay until the guy whose job it was to pick it up came along.

Communicating your vision to the team is a constant process. I explain my vision constantly and say, "This is the direction. I want your help to get us there." The team has to understand the vision, be enthusiastic about it, and be committed to it. So we start the team members off on the right track and rein-force it every day. It works better to do it in short doses than in a lecture.

In a daily meeting we talk briefly about some phase of the image we want. It is important to find ways to reinforce the vision, and to do it constantly. We try to show video clips of players who illustrate an aspect of the vision. We use slogans, emblems, codes, and stories to reinforce the vision. We ask experienced team members to reinforce the vision with beginners. Together we build an environment that produces the training and performance that we want.

Sharing and communicating the vision means that the entire team knows how a Trojan behaves when wearing the Trojan uniform.

*To be on this team you have to play with dignity....When you put on a marine uniform, you're sending out a message. You're a marine—take it or leave it... you'll wear the code of that team without exception.[4]*

> *Everyone in the group must share in the image, and it must energize them. They must act in a way that projects that image.*

A football team's life starts in the spring and lasts one year. Each year we help the group develop into the team we have envisioned—the image that we look like when you watch us at the stadium or on TV. It is a unified image that we project. It is built on each player's image of himself as a member of the group.

Projecting the image of a winner comes partly from winning and knowing that they can win, and partly from being taught how to behave as winners. When players know they can win, they start projecting a winning image, which makes winning in the future more likely. It is a two-way thing, an energy that goes back and forth between the vision and the realization.

## Imagery Mentor[5]

Apparently, many people listen to an inner voice for guidance. For instance, General Douglas MacArthur supposedly conjured up his hero-father for advice on military strategy. The poet Milton called his inner guide "Celestial Patroness" and described how she helped him compose his writings.

In *Thinker Toys*, Michael Michalko suggests one way to access your subconscious and create a personal, internal mentor. Here's a modified version of his procedure:

It is difficult to fathom the full potential of the human mind and especially the subconscious. We must begin to appreciate its ability to help us resolve problems. Imagery Mentor is a good start.

1. Release all your tension and try to relax as much as possible.

2. Visualize a soft, glowing white light surrounding your body. Allow the light to make you feel secure and comfortable.

3. Think of your favorite place (house, mountain, forest, stream, boat). Visualize yourself walking into this place. Notice all the details. Try to imagine what it looks like. Experience any sounds, textures, or smells. Absorb as much as you can.

4. Imagine your personal mentor walking toward you. Look closely at his or her face. What are you experiencing? Think of any special feelings or emotions. Include as much detail as possible.

5. Say to your mentor, "Please be my guide and help me think of new ideas. Lead me in resolving my problem."

6. Tell your mentor about your problem. Give him or her as much relevant information as you can.

   Try to keep your interaction realistic. Listen carefully whenever your mentor speaks to you. Don't be discouraged if ideas don't pop out suddenly. It takes time.

7. Write down any ideas generated during this process. Then end your conversation. Have your mentor say that he or she will be available whenever needed. Experience bonds of trust with your mentor.

# REHEARSAL VISION

Rehearsal vision is tied into an event and our performance in that event. It is a common skill practiced by successful athletes. Greg Louganis, the Olympic diving champion, mentally rehearsed each dive forty times just prior to the dive. Each vision was tied to a specific dive in a specific event.

Rehearsal vision helps me prepare for events that must be taken in stride. I constantly go from one event to the next with little preparation time. I find myself rehearsing an event while driving in the car or riding in an elevator. The ability to see an event in detail, with all the things that can happen, gives me more confidence. Anticipating a meeting with Joe Smith, for example, reminds me of details about him—where his kid attends college, his last vacation, etc. Remembering these

*Rehearsal vision is a type of planning that focuses on the whole performance, not just the script.*

things makes me feel more comfortable and helps me reflect on what we will talk about. Without this preparation, I will not consider details that will enhance our meeting.

Rehearsal vision is a type of planning that focuses on the whole performance, not just the script. I may have a speech in the morning. The next day there may be another speech, the following day two speeches. These are events for which there is no time to sit down and plan. Even if there was the time, I do not plan well sitting at my desk. The speeches may all be similar, but the circumstances are always unique. My preparation is visual, a mental rehearsal about how the event will go. I want to project myself into the event, to see what everyone is wearing, to feel the temperature of the room, to imagine the location of the light switch and thermostat. For a meeting downtown with the mayor, I rehearse what I know about him, what we talked about before, what we might talk about this time, what questions he might ask. Imagining what he will wear suggests how I should dress. It may even remind me that the right suit is at the cleaners and needs to be retrieved.

A key requirement of rehearsal vision for me is the post-game press conference. We have all seen people react badly under stress at press conferences, while others do amazingly well. Walking in cold can be disastrous. In the five minutes it takes to walk off the field after the game, my mind fast-forwards into the media event, anticipating the kinds of questions people will ask and rehearsing the themes and the attitude that I want to project.

UPI/Bettmann

*John Robinson looks forward to meeting the press after the Rams clinch the NFC West title in 1985.*

Rehearsal vision is a skill that people use whether they are aware of it or not. How many times have you left a conversation, imagining what you should have said, how you should have reacted? This is rehearsal vision, focused backwards! Refocus on events in the future and project yourself into those. People who perform well under pressure have the ability to place themselves into situations through visualization.

If the event is important enough, it is easy to spend the time visualizing possibilities and how you will feel about them. There is never enough time to do this in one sitting, so you have to be able to do it in snatches and on the move. If we are playing a game on Saturday, I have already played the game five different ways in rehearsal vision: we win big, we win close, what happens if we lose.... By anticipating what will happen, I can visualize different responses and avoid surprises.

Something that we did at training camp exemplifies the kind of disaster that can happen in the absence of rehearsal vision. We wanted our food service closer to the field to make it more convenient, so we set up a tented area outside. We planned extensively for it. But we failed to visualize—picnic, outdoors, food...flies. We did not see it and feel it. Another problem was that the players coming up from practice were hot, and they never got to really cool down. And, of course, the flies. Visualizing this event again, it is clear what has to change. This year I see that it is cool, the food is good, the players are relaxed...and there are no flies!

## Summary

Vision is the key to growth and accomplishment—in one's personal life and business life.

In life, the ability to dream about the future, what we want to be, and how we want to live—our life vision—has a powerful guiding influence on the choices that we make.

In our jobs, vision provides the same guidance. This "make-something-happen" vision must be shared with the team and evolve to become ours. This vision is more strategic in nature.

The last type of vision, which I call rehearsal vision, helps us to positively anticipate any event, so that when it occurs, we can perform the way we want to.

$O$n a show about the Winter Olympics, someone with a great creative mind edited all of Bonnie Blair's thank you speeches. [American athlete Bonnie Blair's five Olympic gold medals are a speed-skating record.] In every excerpt she says with an incredibly animated face, "I love to skate!" In response to every remark by a commentator, "Congratulations on this tremendous achievement" or "You overcame so many obstacles," Bonnie Blair's response was always the same, "I love to skate."

If you love the process and are obsessed with doing things better, you, too, can go for the gold.

# You Have to Love It

---

**2**

## Love What You Do

Enjoying something requires two things:

1. It has to be something you are good at.

2. You have to try to become an expert in it.

People usually enjoy what they are good at. Knowing what your talents are is the first step. Then, over time, you need to develop your talent to become an expert in your skill—the best public speaker, the most skilled surgeon, the foremost chair builder—whatever. In your quest, you need to seek knowledge. In the preceding

*Coaches have the opportunity to help people develop talent in such a way that they can increase their enjoyment of it as well as their mastery over it.*

examples, you would seek knowledge about the art of speaking to groups, of performing surgery, or of building chairs. Look to others for guidance and feedback. Develop an appreciation for the "art" of what you do.

Teaching the skill can greatly increase your awareness of the elements that contribute to greatness in the skill. A great chair builder or cabinetmaker may not be able to articulate what is involved in the art of his craft. He may not consciously be aware of what creates or contributes to his competence. But he can model what he does and talk about the experience. When someone exhibits the expertise we seek to develop, we appreciate and want to learn from his example.

### WHAT IS ENJOYMENT?

Reuters/Bettmann

*American speed skater Bonnie Blair celebrates after the crowd roared her on to a 500-meter gold medal and a rink record in the 1992 Albertville, France, Olympics.*

Some people are not attuned to the source of their enjoyment. It is important to be able to say "I enjoy this" or "I don't enjoy that." Define the enjoyment so you have a sense of "I like doing this"; "I'm good at this"; "I enjoy being involved with other people"; "I enjoy working with these tools." Coaches have the opportunity to help people develop talent in such a way that they can increase their enjoyment of it as well as their mastery over it.

Enjoyment is different from pleasure. Pleasure has a receiving connotation to it; it does not take commitment or work. When I speak of "enjoyment," I mean that the participant is actively involved and there must be a reason or objective for the activity. It is a task that requires that you bring something to it, and it demands effort. The result of the activity must be some kind of measurable achievement, whether you are trying to build a chair, arrive at a conclusion, or make a deal. And your goal must be challenging. Building a thousand chairs the same way does not involve any challenge, but constantly trying to improve the process does.

John Gardner, founder of Common Cause, commented that

> *"Everyone has noted the astonishing*
> *sources of energy that seem available*
> *to those who enjoy what they are doing, who*
> *find meaning in what they are doing.*
> *The self-renewing man knows that if he has*
> *no great conviction about what he is doing,*
> *he had better find something*
> *that he can have great conviction about..."*[1]

Some people would not characterize it as enjoyment or having "fun"—they might call it commitment , dedication, or perseverance. I call it enjoyment or loving what you do. Whatever it is—and it is not goal-oriented— springs from who you are, what you have a talent for, what you enjoy, what you bring to the job on a daily basis, and what you take home on a daily basis.

Building enjoyment takes mental discipline and a focus on doing the process well. It requires that you spend time thinking about what you do and how you do it. As you go about your job, check your enjoyment. That involves finding the things that absorb you, that make time fly. When you say, "I had a great day today. We had four problems, but it was exciting," you know that you are having fun.

Loving what you do helps you become better at it; mastery is an ongoing process. The people who I regard as tremendously successful all have this. There is a certain energy or a joy in the process of doing it as opposed to the

*Remember the process rather than the prize.*

achievement. The process is the important part. If you work on the process, the results will follow. Remember the process rather than the prize. Without dedication to the process, you will never achieve your potential.

We all need to set goals and have a vision. Yet, if we are not careful, the goal-oriented career can become a Bataan Death March as opposed to "Boy, do I like going to work today."

## ENJOYMENT BUILDS ENERGY

People who are the best at what they do possess joy in going to work. People who love their work don't have a problem getting up or being on time; their day races by. When you feel energetic, you're ready to take on new challenges. If you enjoy something, you can't give it up.

In his book, *Flow: The Psychology of Optimal Experience*, Mihaly Czikszentmihalyi discussess this state of mind and experience when things are going great. At such times, we become so involved in the process of what we are doing that we have an almost euphoric feeling. Czikszentmihalyi describes it as losing track of time, losing track of self, being totally absorbed in what you are doing and in each element of that. Everyone has shared the experience of being totally absorbed in an activity, then wondering, "Where did the day go?"

That is what I want our football players to experience. The fun I talk about in playing football is the enjoyment that causes our players to want to become better, to want to repeat the experience.

It is ridiculous to assume that one might feel this way all of the time on the job. We all have things we do not like about our jobs. However, when people are doing the right job and working at it in the right way, they find the experience fulfilling, satisfying, and enjoyable

*USC Sports Information*

*"I know one thing. If I wasn't enjoying it, I'd get out."*[2]

85 percent of the time. Fifteen percent of the job may be tedious, but those are the dues we pay. We get the boring part over with so that we can really enjoy the other part.

## RESPECT YOUR GIFT

Unless they are narrow-minded, most people recognize the value of other talents—the value of being an actor, or a painter, or a mathematician. It may be one of the real signs of ignorance to be unable to see the value of diverse human endeavors, to not have respect for people who possess different gifts. That's a foolish prejudice that I have very little patience with. It is very disappointing if you possess a gift and—through indifference or because no one around you values it—you do not respect or develop it.

Many people realize their strengths through example or encouragement. Being able to recognize a gift and being willing to pursue the maximum of your capabilities is one of life's big obligations. We have other obligations, obviously, but that is an important and fundamental one. Gifts are just that. They are not ours through any credit of our own.

If you are going to enjoy what you do, start by accepting yourself and building on your own strengths. Evaluate yourself so that you understand your strengths and weaknesses. Coaches work with people as they are. They help people develop the talent that is there.

## RESPECT DIFFERENCES

Make a plan based on what you're good at. Unfortunately, some people think that what they are good at is trivial. They think they should embrace things that others think are more meaningful. Rather than change yourself, change what you do. If you don't care about your marketing job and would love to be an iron worker, do it! Do what you're good at. Then seek to excel at it.

# Time to Know All About FLOW

## Dr. Mihaly Czikszentmihalyi, University of Chicago

**What do you call this state of involvement and concentration?**

Flow Experience is the name that I've given it. So many people use the analogy of flowing, being carried away by a force that makes whatever they're doing seem effortless and automatic.

Flow differs from peak performance and other states in that it's an end in itself. You don't go into the Flow state in order to accomplish something else—like psyching up athletes so they can win a game.

...Flow Experience takes a lot of work—athletes must go through grueling workouts and artists must study for years—to achieve that state.

**Do you have to be an artist or an athlete to experience Flow?**

No. Between 85% and 90% of the people I interviewed said that they had had the feeling at one time or another— sometimes on the job, sometimes at home, playing with the kids. They say these are the most enjoyable moments in their lives.

**How can people learn to achieve Flow?**

The most important thing is to find the right place to start. Some people who decide to write a novel just do it. For most of us, however, it's better to start with something less daunting, like a few short stories. If you leap in over your head, you'll wind up frustrated. Better: take on something you think you can handle but that has the potential of becoming more and more complex as you go along...

**What else is needed to achieve Flow?**

You have to get over your sense of self-consciousness. Being self-conscious prevents you from concentrating on anything except yourself.

There also must be a meeting of challenges and skills.

The transition into a state of Flow can be very difficult—even painful.

Example: People who write professionally often have to go through a devastating hour or two where they psych themselves up to forget everything else so they can get immersed in what they're doing.

**Are there any tricks that can make it easier to achieve Flow?**

Some people use rituals to put their mind on automatic pilot and ease them into a state of concentration.

This is only possible if you're totally absorbed in what you're doing at all times, if your personal life and your work life have merged. When this happens, you're always essentially in the same world...you don't have to make the tough transitions back and forth. I would think that for some highly creative people, the occasional transition into what most of us think of as real life would be a painful one.

**What kind of people have difficulty reaching a state of Flow?**

People who don't like to take risks have a hard time achieving Flow.

Most people are afraid to move away from the routine activities that they know they can control. Their fear comes from a lack of self-confidence.

When you're engaged in a Flow activity, you're stretching yourself and putting yourself on the line. The challenges are more difficult than those you usually encounter and you feel your skills are barely adequate.

That's why most people prefer to do very safe things. Nothing strange or bad can happen while you're watching TV. On the other hand, nothing very good will happen either.

*Reprinted with permission of Bottom Line/Personal, 55 Railroad Avenue, Greenwich, CT 06830*

If you are a left-brained, organized, persevering person, perseverance ought to be part of what you plan to do with your life. If you are not creative, do not aim at becoming the creative director of an advertising firm. And if you are a creative person, do not obsess about being disorganized; accept that you are not going to be organized. I am not organized, so I find people who balance my weakness and who provide help with organization. I do not want the people I coach to focus on the negative but instead to think "If I do what I'm capable of, I can make it."

## Effective Teaching

Coaches need to accommodate the differences in how people learn. Obviously, some people learn faster than others, and many learn in different ways. To help a person develop his talent, find out how that person learns. Some people are very physical and learn best when they see a skill demonstrated. Their understanding of what is required is kinesthetic; they learn faster if it is explained first, then demonstrated. For these players, the words must make sense or the actions never will.

Making learning fun is something coaches must master. Learning the skill should be fun; it should not be negative. Teaching can make a subject dull or exciting. If you teach history, you can make learning about World War II one of the most fascinating things in the world or just a jumble of dates and places—"D-day was June 6, 1944," etc. I had a college professor who taught history in terms of the people. He made Napoleon come alive. We attended his lectures as if they were entertainment! You had to fight to get in his class. That is the kind of teaching that I am talking about. As a coach, try to constantly create situations where the group learns more—about skills, the job, the overall mission of the company. This is essential and ongoing.

*You are really never playing against an opponent. You are playing against yourself, your own highest standards. And when you reach your limits, that is real joy.*

—Arthur Ashe

## THE ENJOYMENT IS IN THE PROCESS

Care about the tools you use. If words are your tools, care about words. If your tool is a hammer, care about that hammer. Growing up, I was a carpenter's assistant one year. The carpenter took great care of his tools. When I do a home repair job, I lose my tools because I do not care about the skills that go with them; I neither excel at nor enjoy handyman skills. I will throw a hammer somewhere and then wonder, "Where did that hammer go?" as if it took off by itself. The great carpenter values and never loses his tools.

A respect for the process we are involved with increases our capacity to love it. First of all, we respect the act. We believe that it has significance. When we start something that we value, our enjoyment may be quite small. Nurtured over a period of years, the enjoyment increases tenfold. The older you are, the more you rely on the satisfaction you get from seeking to excel. As you get better at something, you love it more. As you advance, you understand it more. You have more control of the skills and are coming to understand greatness a little better. Your knowledge is better. You have seen greatness and can appreciate the skills of others and see the vastness that remains for you to accomplish. So commitment is important to increasing your enjoyment. It is vital that you have a sense of the importance of doing your job well, of giving it your best effort.

When the season is over and you have accomplished your goal, you have to remind people where the fun really was. Was it the announcement of the sales figures for the quarter that told us that we won, or was it in devising and executing the winning strategy? Was being ranked number one the fun, or was doing it the fun?

When people reminisce about great times, they tell stories about parts of the process—staying up late to meet a deadline, tackling an impossible problem and finding the solution. It is while we are actively engaged in the process that we have the most enjoyment; that is where the real joy resides. And that does not diminish the importance of goals at all.

## Encourage Risk Taking

Environments that succeed are where people have fun doing it and are willing to take risks. Being willing to take risks is really important. The environment must encourage risk taking. That means that it supports the unsuccessful effort. Coaches can encourage risk taking and give support when it does not work by saying, "Let's evaluate what happened here." Losing is a big part of winning.

> *A*round here, one of the examples we set is that you can have fun, you can make jokes.
>
> —Herb Kelleher
> on working at
> Southwest Airlines

The lessons from failures are often the keys to success. When someone knows that he is not going to get his head chopped off for trying unsuccessfully, there is a greater willingness to put oneself on the line.

Some risks—those you are not prepared for—are just stupid. I love to take risks in football, when I know that I have evaluated the situation and judged that this is the right time.

## DON'T OUTGROW YOUR STRENGTHS

It is important to remain focused on your strengths and the sources of your enjoyment as your career advances. In coaching, the head coach at times becomes the major problem solver. He coaches the coaches and often abandons the thing he enjoyed so much—coaching the player. As you advance in your career, avoid this pitfall.

One of the things that happens when people are promoted is that many of the skills that they developed and enjoyed using are no longer required of them as leaders. Someone who enjoyed team camaraderie may lose that when he takes an executive office. It is important if you change jobs to remember where your satisfaction comes from and to retain aspects of that in the new position. As you assume the duties of the new job, reshape it to fit who you are. If you are an engineer and they make you the leader, you ought to lead from an engineering standpoint. You ought to still have your sleeves rolled up. If you need to have a desk on the executive floor but keep another in the lab, the shop, or the assembly area. You cannot allow yourself to become simply the problem solver or administrator unless those things also give you satisfaction. Without that enjoyment you are robbing yourself of the energy that got you where you are now. We always have to acknowledge who we are and what we do well. Ask yourself, "Am I using my strengths? Do I enjoy what I am doing?"

*My father ran a production operation of several hundred workers. He had two offices, one up with the other executives and another right off the production floor. He spent more time with the workers than with the executives. He was an early example of a leader as coach.*[3]

"Advancement" may require developing new skills—we never stop doing that. Still, when I am driving home I know that the primary enjoyment I get in my job is from coaching. If I don't do very much of that in a day, I don't have as much fun. But if I get involved in planning or if I am with the players in some way, then I have a good day. I have gone through periods where I have not been involved as a coach or a teacher. Then I become less than I was. Every leader has to do the things that nourish him. If you are good at it, and that is where you came from, do not lose those roots.

## PAY ATTENTION WHEN YOU ARE NOT HAVING FUN

In most of my career, I have felt very good about what I have been doing. But I went through a period that taught me more about this than all of the good years. I coached the L. A. Rams for nine years; we had seven successful years, then two very bad ones. Our program just fell apart, and I was fired. The thing that really stuck out as I went through that process was how my outlook changed. Was it a cause or was it effect? Many things were causes. I do know that, in the process of the ship sinking, I no longer enjoyed it. As a result, I no longer brought to my job the ability to right the ship. As the ship was going down, so was I. And then I was much less of what I think I am, than I should have been. The question for me was what I needed to do to get back the enjoyment.

©*Peter Read Miller/NFL Photos*

*Robinson coached the NFL's Los Angeles Rams (1983-1991) to a 79-74 mark—the most wins of any Rams head coach. He reached the playoffs 6 times, twice advancing to the NFC championship game (1985 and 1989).* [4]

## SUMMARY

Enjoying what you do starts with figuring out what you are good at; your greatest enjoyment is usually linked to your greatest strengths.

Enjoyment increases as our dedication and skill level increases. This enjoyment is a wellspring of energy that discounts efforts required, difficulties that may arise, or setbacks that must be endured. It makes us unaware of time, enthusiastic about our calling, disbelieving at times that this could be called "work."

*F*ocusing on the process is just as important as having a vision and loving what you do. In fact, focusing on the process is what makes it possible to achieve our vision and to build enjoyment in our talent. The process of developing a talent is easy. We get positive feedback about the skills we develop. That encourages us to try harder. Results and enjoyment make the effort rewarding and fun; the sacrifices it entails are unimportant. Focusing on the process and seeking results are not conflicting goals; they get strength from each other.

# FOCUS ON THE PROCESS

**3**

*Total performance of excellence is a flow of behavior,
when there are no conscious steps
in the mind of the performer.
Studies we have conducted of the best basketball players
tell us when they do a slam dunk
or another of their very best plays
they act almost unconsciously.
They are on automatic, at one with the activity.
The clock doesn't tick.*

Donald O. Clifton and Paula Nelson,
*Soar With Your Strengths*

## PROCESS VS. GOALS

In any effort, success if very important. You want to win.
I have little patience with people who minimize the
importance of winning; particularly in sports, the idea
of playing the game is to win. Yet we can cheat ourselves
out of enjoyment of the process if we place too great an
emphasis on a mindset of "We must win this...." John
Wooden, the great former UCLA basketball coach,

stressed the idea of achieving your best by focusing on self-improvement versus a goal of winning. Enjoying the process and playing a game against a challenging competitor is very important. The desire to win drives us to higher performance levels, and enjoyment of the process helps us achieve those levels. Balancing these two is the key.

The relationship between goals and process can be compared to a road trip that leads us to our destination. The process is the freeway, the goals are the little towns along the way. Each goal is important, but it is not the end of the journey. The process sustains you as you reach each goal. The effort you put into the journey is what advances you to each stop along the way. Winning comes at the end. Doing the process right is the key to winning. Goals are great when they are viewed this way. The process is what allows us to advance from level to level of skill mastery. It is never over. Anyone can restart the process.

## DON'T FOCUS ON THE RESULT

Companies often make the mistake of overemphasizing the bottom line. They encourage results-oriented behavior with slogans like "We've got 20 more to go!" Graphics are used to illustrate the shrinking gap between targeted and actual results. This can be exciting, but I suspect that it also encourages people to stop as soon as the gap closes. People pause when they say, "We did it!" They relax as opposed to saying, "That was great. Next time I'll develop a better presentation." That's the problem with too great a focus on goals—it encourages stops and starts in effort. The process of continually improving our skills and competitiveness is never over. Organizations that focus exclusively on annual or quarterly goals prevent themselves from finding out how good they can be, how much they can achieve.

Champions concentrate on becoming the best they can be rather than on winning the prize. Each competition is viewed as a challenge and an opportunity to do their best. In the end, such individuals and organizations win more, and they win more often. When you are involved in a contest of any kind—a football game, a product launching, a sales presentation—the excitement is in the struggle, in making progress.

The thrill that comes from pushing a well-honed skill to its limits in close competition is what drives us to want to go out and do it again. Goals, seen this way, spur us along. "We did really well" has a finality to it. "How can we do this even better?" keeps people moving forward. Unfortunately our society tends to reinforce a winner-take-all mentality toward competition, which teaches our players that goals are the target. This minimizes the importance of using both experiences—success and failure—for performance improvement.

The young people that I coach at USC all have hopes and dreams of success—to be first-string, to be an All-American, to be drafted by the NFL, to make a lot of money in a professional career, to have Michael Jordan's advertising contracts—as well as the desire to be part of a national championship team. These are the dreams they test when they play with us. Not all of them will achieve 100 percent of all they desire, but they won't know if they are not willing to try.

> *What success takes is trying one's best to the limits of one's talent.*

## LEARNING TO TRY HARD

When you approach something, approach it with a sense of its importance and a sense of commitment to doing it well. People have to learn to give of themselves in this way. It takes years to learn to give our best efforts. That is the major difference in the young employee who joins a firm and the more mature employee. The young person's intellect may equal his elder's, but the young person's ability to give his best effort is limited because he is untrained and undisciplined.

*S*uccess is a journey, not a destination.

—Ben Sweetland

The same is true with a young athlete; he just does not know how to try his hardest. When somebody says, "I'm trying my hardest," it may mean that it is the hardest that person can try today, but in reality it may represent 60 percent of the person's total capacity. Over time, anyone can improve. The desire lies in believing "I can do this better," "I will improve." If you want to build better chairs, your thousandth chair will be better than your first. Hopefully you are obsessed with it. You know your two thousandth chair will be tremendously better than you one thousandth.

Developing an interest in the process is part of what they call becoming a pro. A coach can fan that interest by outlining the skills needed, then pointing out the skills the player has and the ones that must be developed. The coach shows what must be done in order to accomplish the desired level of excellence.

Most players who come to us have experienced some success. As a result, they may have a distorted belief about what it takes to succeed. What success takes is trying one's best to the limits of one's talent; we will teach them what that requires and hope they become consumed in the process.

In training camp we temporarily eliminate all other aspects of a person's life. We create a situation where they must be totally involved in the team. They work seventeen hours a day. Under that kind of pressure, almost everyone thinks of quitting. Their endurance and their ability to concentrate are stretched. They must measure up to a certain standard. They must measure up to their peers' expectations. You cannot be the guy that falls out! They learn a lot about trying hard and persevering.

They may have no idea how many muscles can hurt, how tired they can become, how much stamina they have got. They may start to wonder, "What about my personal life? What about my weekends?" We must teach not only the required job skills, but also the level of commitment necessary to succeed.

## BUILD CONFIDENCE, BUILD SUCCESS

When we're new at anything, a natural first thought is "Can I do this? Can I be a part of this team?" One of the major roles of the coach is to help players say, "I can do it!" Give the player time to build his confidence. One way to do that is to build on success. We start by giving people tasks they can perform. We put them in an environment where they will succeed. We do not ask people to do things we know they are not good at. This can only lead to embarrassment and failure—and it is hard to see who that will benefit. We don't get hung up on what they can't do or on their bad habits. Initially, we protect them from weak or problem areas.

*USC Sports Information*

*When Marcus Allen won the Heisman Trophy in 1981, he set 14 new NCAA records and tied two others.*

Along with confidence comes a greater willingness to take risks and to tackle new challenges. Now they are ready to ask the next question, "How can I excel? How do I get to be the best?" Each player wants to learn how to become really great in their strengths, and to perform acceptably in those things that they don't do very well. That is the beginning of the road to greatness. Anyone

*It is the preparation that gives you the edge.*

who is going to grow must push the limits of his performance and develop the skills that surround the core activity that he is good at, that he feels good about, and that he thrives on.

Without the experience of success, the willingness to take risks is not there. We see that in athletes who do not have confidence in the academic classroom. They do not feel like they can master the topics, so they cut class because they feel bad when they go. Our hope is that young players come out of their first season thinking they are pretty darned good. We want them to have a sense that they *can* succeed.

Players with a strong belief in their own skills develop resilience, an ability to rebound after setbacks. It is that confidence that gives them the strength to get up and keep going when they have been knocked down. Without confidence they cannot keep exerting the maximum effort. Without confidence they are of no value to the team.

Building on each player's foundation helps him become resilient. He has a sense of self-worth and a belief that he can learn to be better. If I am shooting baskets and I have missed the last ten, it takes confidence to believe that I am really pretty good at this, and that if I keep shooting, I'll make the next ten. That kind of a belief is nurtured through a growing skill level, the enthusiasm of coaches, and the support of teammates. That belief sustains the player and allows him to keep going.

## PHYSICAL CONDITIONING

Between spring practice and training camp, we develop tailored summer conditioning for each player. This conditioning can raise the level of the person's performance significantly. There are different kinds of players.

Defensive backs are like racehorses; their job is to run and run and run. They are lean, highly skilled fast guys. They can run forever and never get tired. Their problem becomes pulled muscles. Without the right kind of conditioning, they can have a muscle go all of a sudden. For a defensive lineman, conditioning is a whole different thing. His cardiovascular endurance does not have to be so good. He gets tired. When we analyzed the area a lineman has to play in, we decided it was about a twelve-yard radius. We use a big rope to illustrate his running radius. Now strength is something else. He has got to be strong. Conditioning for him requires muscular development and building strength. He does a lot of weight training. This conditioning leads to a better level of performance, fewer injuries, and better performance under pressure.

*The way you become more of a competitor is through skill development and conditioning.*

The off-season is really important for us because that is when we develop our hand. We play the cards in the season. Whether you have aces in your hand is developed in the off-season. They don't give you new cards during the season; those cards are dealt. The season is how well you play your hand. You may get a little bit of a re-deal—something happens to an opponent, for example—but not much. The season is the execution. That is true in most endeavors. Talent and conditioning are developed before you have to compete. It is the preparation that gives you the edge.

## IT'S A SKILL PROBLEM!

There is a lot of talk in sports about choking or not coming through in the clutch. A baseball batter strikes out and it is attributed to being in a clutch, as if there is something wrong with him psychologically! In reality, the pitcher threw him a curve ball and the batter does not hit curve balls. When the player learns to hit curve balls, he has not only gained psychological stamina but also has improved his skills. Now, if they throw him a fast ball and he hits that, you can say, "Boy, he came through"; which he did, in good part, because he possesses that skills. As coaches we must take what goes wrong down to a skill level and a level of preparation. The more skilled you are, the better you can focus on the act. The way you become more of a competitor is through skill development and conditioning.

## LEARNING SKILLS

UPI/Bettmann

*Los Angeles Rams coach encourages running back Eric Dickerson (#29) during a workout at practice.*

When a task is beyond our capabilities, we feel frustrated. Coaching the skill required to master a task will make the process of playing more fulfilling and will encourage the person to excel.

When players come to us, they may be unaware of what they need to do to improve. A player with great speed who cannot change direction may have succeeded until now because he is so fast. When you talk about the need to change direction faster, he wonders what you are talking about. As a coach you must lead him to the point where he begins to say "Oh, that's what you mean!"

We spend a lot of time coaching specific skill drills and basic plays: throwing and catching the ball, blocking, tackling, running for maximum speed. Teaching skills is doable. We can analyze and make improvements there. We do not tolerate a player saying, "I've got it now. Let's go on to a new set of skills." The core skills must be practiced every day to become sharp and stay sharp.

Teaching these skills can be a challenge. As a coaching staff we talk about that a lot! You tell him and you tell him and he nods. You say, "You got that?" and he says, "I got it." Then somewhere down the road—maybe a week or two later—he asks, "Oh, is this what you mean?" People pretend they understand when they do not, so you cannot take agreement too seriously.

## GET FEEDBACK

Teachers tend to supply answers. We say, "2 + 2 is 4. Right?" And we get the answer, "Right." We don't work hard enough at getting feedback or at making the person verify understanding. Make him say "2 + 2 is 4" Then ask, "What's a 4?"

Test understanding. Get the person to give back information to you or demonstrate that he understands. Getting feedback and checking understanding used to be the key for John Madden. He would describe a week's preparation as follows: First he would stand and the players at, while he did all of the talking. Next, he would sit with the players, and they would talk back and forth. Finally, the player would stand and tell him what he was going to do, as John sat and listened. When that process happened, John felt comfortable.

*T*he person with a singular ability often does not have respect for or interest in things outside his area of expertise. The person may be fearful about attempting skills in other areas. We give players some time to acquire new habits..

# LEARNING TO WORK WITH OTHERS

While a lot of skill development is an individual responsibility, the player must also learn how to be a team member. Our players have four or five years to establish the ethic of dedicating themselves to the development of

Focus On Sports

*"Soloists are inspiring in opera and perhaps even in small entrepreneurial ventures, but there is no place for them in large corporations."*

—Norman R. Augustine
President and CEO, Martin Marietta Corp.

their talents and their ability to be good team members. We use mentoring to help with this, without defining it as such. It is different from the mentor each player gets on the academic side, which is quite structured. Team mentors are more informal. Our people have to possess an almost missionary zeal when it comes to encouraging new members to put in the required effort. They are enthusiastic about talking to the new teammate and showing him the ropes. This bonding and shared indoctrination reinforces the point of everyone being engaged in a common cause. The group acknowledges its shared responsibility to help new team members adopt our ethic.

The person with a singular ability often does not have respect for or interest in things outside his area of expertise. The person may be fearful about attempting skills in other areas. We give players some time to acquire new habits.

For a while we may tolerate the fact that he violates our code; he does not understand it yet. The team helps the individual learn that even if he is the greatest, an enormous talent, he will not succeed if he does not follow our code. But together we will teach him. We coach the group to accept this responsibility. We are the team, we want these new members to help us. They have got something to offer that we need and we want. It is part of our code to bring this new team member along.

In addition to getting a lot of work done in a short time, a bonding occurs in training camp. We are allowed about eigtheen days, and we try to cram a lot in. All players are pushed to their limits. Any time a group is subjected to adversity, as training camp inevitably is, there is a coming together of that group, a bonding that occurs. Players are tired. They are homesick. The training is nonstop. Everyone begins to take a step closer to the man next to him. They have a sense of having endured a rite of passage and of being in this together.

Teamwork is rewarding when people realize that they can learn a lot from others. They learn from being with people who stand for something. In a sales team, people learn from the successful proposals others have written. Programmers want to examine computer codes that someone else has built. Manufacturing workers who have figured out a way to improve time or quality on the line find others are curious about it. Players want to analyze their teammates' plays to see if they can learn something that will improve their own performance. That is the type of involvement that leads to continuous improvement. It does not have stops and starts in it—and in the end, it is more successful.

## UNDERSTANDING THE MENTAL GAME

Football is obviously a game of mental strategies, but a less obvious mental aspect is how we control our emotions. Well-prepared and focused players are not too emotional before the game. Emotion does not win.

> *A preparation that is too emotional*
> *may not have enough substance to it.*
> *You are not really ready to compete;*
> *you are only ready*
> *to have an adrenaline flow.*
> *When the adrenaline flow wears off,*
> *about halfway through the game,*
> *you are left without the tactics*
> *and the plan you need to win.*

*The great performer is, first of all, a great preparation person.*

Being ready to compete to win the game starts with preparation—good strategies, well-developed skills, and, of course, teamwork.

Some people talk about a player who rises to the occasion, who only plays great in games. That is a myth. There is not anybody who is lazy, indifferent, casual, and a cool guy during the week who is suddenly transformed on game day. It does not happen. There is no mental process that could transform such a player. It is the talented player who prepares during the week, who works at it, who does the things that he needs to do to prepare himself that has the opportunity to play well. The great performer is, first of all, a great preparation person.

There may be people who are so mellow and "in the flow" during the week that you may misinterpret enjoyment for lack of effort. This is a lack of strain, not a lack of effort. They don't seem to be exerting themselves. This is what we mean by hard not being painful.

*As a coach, you need know your players well enough to be able to distinguish who is fully involved and who can do more.*

Fear affects performance. Being scared of the possibility of failure is healthy. It can mobilize us to action. Successful people respond to that. They do not let it become the kind of fear that immobilizes them. The importance of the event can add to your fear. You really want that goal. What if you make an error? If this fear puts your brain on the wrong wavelength, you cannot think ahead. Your ability to use rehearsal vision is shut down. Fear makes you jittery.

In a performance of any kind—a game, a play, a sales presentation—you need to be able to say, "I know what to do; I know the process here. I'm really ready." That confidence helps you deal with fear. You can visualize what is going to happen or what might happen. Find a way to visualize the event and to keep yourself within the process. Your brain in rehearsal vision cannot think of two things at once. So the immobilizing fear stops. It helps if you think, "This isn't such a big deal."

In golf tournaments, winning often comes down to one short putt. The player who lines up the ball and says to himself, "This is for the title!" has no chance of making it. On the other hand, a player's performance flows if he can say, "I feel the rhythm in my arms. I love putting. I see the hole. It's that big. When I complete my stroke, I see it go in." Being in the flow of the process gives you better concentration, slower breathing, and more relaxed muscles.

*Focus On Sports*

*Ben Crenshaw at the 1993 Masters.*

When a player seems to make great plays, he is confident in his skills, not worried about outcomes. He is able to get into that zone where he loses track of himself, where he is totally immersed. Great plays happen when you are into the game, not worried about the result, and feeling good. You are stimulated, not worried, by the pressure. It is part of what energizes you. The focus is not on the outcome; the focus is on the performance.

When people become really great, they begin to see things in slow motion. The average person sees a tennis ball that is going to hit them; the really great tennis player sees it differently. He sees it coming in an arc and bouncing in this precise spot. The baseball player sees the spin on the seam of the ball. That is what is meant by being in the flow or in the zone. You are tuned into it. Helping players reach that experience involves their dedication to learning the basics, trying hard, dedication and developing their talent.

## Beyond Winning and Losing

Great players know that the game's never over. Even when you lose, you get to play again next week. Of course some things are final, like goals. But the process is never over. In most cases that sense of keeping going has value. One of the keys to successful performance is to forget the last success, to forget the last failure. If there is any memory, it should be of how it felt during moments of flow, and the desire to get there again. Focus on the process rather than the prize. That is where the enjoyment is, where the essence is.

## SUMMARY

As a coach, you have the opportunity to help people develop talent in such a way that they can increase their enjoyment of it as well as their mastery over it. Our players also develop tremendous life skills—the habit of applying themselves to a personal responsibility, showing respect for others, being prepared, giving their best effort, constantly improving their skills, and following through.

# PART TWO

*E*ach year the team is new. Each team has a character of its own. Talent distinguishes the best teams. Morale, spirit, and teamwork are important, but you need talent to win. To become champions, the team must first be talented, then it must refine that talent into the right skills and the right habits. The skills must be those needed to defeat your opponents. And the strategies the team relies on most heavily must play to those strengths.

# DEVELOPING A
# WINNING
# ORGANIZATION

*For many, their experiences as part of
truly great teams stand out as singular periods
of life lived to the fullest.
Some spend the rest of their lives
looking for ways to recapture that spirit.*

Peter Senge, *The Fifth Discipline*

# 4

## MY IMAGE OF WINNING TEAMS

When I think of championship teams, I think of seasons.
The 1972 USC team, when I was assistant coach to John
McKay, is a good example. The team was a really talented group of individuals who had experienced two 6-4
seasons—disappointing seasons. I joined this group
when they were seniors, ready to win. They were all
hungry that season. They were the most vital group of
people that I have ever been around. They were alive the
whole year. They were so excited about the process that
they would have played two games every Saturday if
we'd let them. We won every game. We won the national championship. We got every vote for the national

*It is the team that wins, not individuals. The great organization develops depth of excellence in every function, just as an excellent football team does.*

champions and were considered one of the two or three great teams of all times. That team had no star. Everyone was pretty good. Prior to that, they had not quite achieved their potential and they were bent on improving.

My ideal situation is to have two good quarterbacks, a good defense, and a good offense, so that we do not have to ask any one person to win for us. The quarterback plays a big role, but this is still a team that he is playing on! We will not ask him to win the game for us. He has a lot of responsibility...like everybody else on the team.

It is a mistake to center too much attention on the quarterback or, in other settings, on a designated leader. Such a team expects to ride on one individual's shoulders to victory. Our 1972 team had two outstanding quarterbacks. But that was not the team's prime focus. These two players played great, but they were not the reason we won. Nobody put an undue amount of responsibility for winning on the quarterbacks.

It is the team that wins, not individuals. Every one needs a role in the outcome. That 1972 team sums up much of what I see as a winning team: talented, growing, intense, and having the desire to win. On that team everyone shared in the responsibility for winning. Everyone believed they had an important role in the result. The burden did not fall on any one player or unit within our group. Each player knew that they could and would contribute, that they had part of the responsibility on their shoulders.

It is the same way in any organization. Many leaders rely on one or two functions, such as engineering, manufacturing, or sales. The great organization develops depth and excellence in every function, just as an excellent football team does. They do not leave it all up to customer relations, accounting, product design, or sales. In winning organizations, the service is excellent, accounting is on the ball, manufacturing is state of the art, administration is superbly efficient.

## EVERYONE HAS A ROLE

Giving everyone a share of the responsibility for the result fosters teamwork. If an organization focuses too much responsibility for winning on certain parts—the offense or the quarterback—it inadvertently fosters a lack of respect for those functions and the people in them. This is destructive. A sense of fairness is essential to fostering shared responsibility. On the player's level, it means giving players of the same caliber equal opportunities to play and to improve. On the functional level, it requires that all functions pull their weight.

Relying too heavily on one group or one person reduces an organization's competitiveness. We have all heard variations along the lines of "If the star salesperson comes through again, we'll make our numbers." That sentiment reflects a lack of respect and creates a dynamic that is harmful to teamwork—an us versus them situation. Such teams often win games and meet sales quotas. But their success is tenuous. There is a tension in their performance. They do not have the energy that comes from shared responsibility—where every

*Reprinted with special permission of King Features Syndicate*

*Heinz Kluetmeier/Sports Illustrated*

*The joy of the US Olympic Hockey team's shared success in their victory over the USSR team is evident.*

function of your team knows it owns part of the responsibility for winning and is held account-able for that contribution. That kind of team tends to operate at a higher level of proficiency.

Being on a fully functioning team is equiv-alent to driving a car with all cylinders firing, flying a plane with all engines functioning, or riding a bicycle with all gears operational. Energy is at a consistently higher level. There is a greater ability to shift pace or adjust strategy. There are greater reserves of power if needed. There is less tension about the outcome. Observing these teams, people describe them as inspired. They are disciplined, dedicated, and highly skilled. These teams have fun!

If I were having a coronary bypass, that is the kind of team I would want performing my heart surgery. If I were an astronaut, that is the kind of team I would want at mission control. In fact, that is the kind of team I hope worked on my car and on every appliance in my house. It is the kind of team I want at my bank, at the restaurants where I eat, and so on.

*I want teams like that all around me, and I want to coach that kind of team: skilled, covering all the bases, working in harmony, happy doing their jobs, and making it seem like no effort at all.*

I also know how hard it is to make such teams happen. It is a function of luck, dedication, and tremendous op-portunity. This is such a rare experience, that once it occurs, people try to recapture it again and again. Building such teams is our challenge. Even when all of the ingredients are there, they require patient and skill-ful handling. With a strong vision guiding you, the right talent, and the right assistant coaches, you can achieve it.

♦ Start with clear and high expectations. People live up or down to our expectations of them.

♦ Clearly define roles and responsibilities.

♦ Make sure that the skills needed for every function are highly developed.

♦ Emphasize that, in every effort, the total team wins and loses; that everyone shares equal responsibility and no one is inferior or superior.

For example, it does not matter whether it is the motherboard or the power supply on your computer that is out; the end result is that it does not work. Nor does it matter whether it is the first or second violin that is playing the sour notes—the sound is equally painful. The entire team achieves the outcome. With mutual respect for each other's contributions, teams generally communicate well. The realization that everyone is focused on a mutually important outcome fosters cooperation. Such teams monitor performance from within.

*The realization that we are focused on a mutually important outcome fosters cooperation. Such teams monitor performance from within.*

A coach can actually be the source of disrespect and friction among team members. Whenever you leave a player's role unclear or ignore his level of proficiency, you convey that what he does is not important. Whenever you single someone out for praise—the quarterback or the chief salesperson—you reinforce that some people are more important than others. If you single out culprits for blame, you communicate that it is not the team as a whole that is responsible but isolated parts of it. The total team wins and the total team loses.

More often than they would like, coaches and managers find themselves in situations where they are flying with a single engine, where the talent of the team is so uneven that they must rely more heavily than they should on single parts of the organization.

© *John E. Biever/NFL Photos*

*A dejected John Elway after Washington's 42-10 victory over Denver in Super Bowl XXII.*

I remember reading a newspaper article, when the Denver Broncos were playing the Washington Redskins in Super Bowl XXII. Denver's coach said something to the effect of, "If we're going to have any chance to win, John Elway has to have a great day." The coach was right. They found themselves in that position. Those were the cards that they were playing with. As we all remember, John did not have a good day, and he is a great player. That type of pressure and responsibility is not the way to motivate any player to have a great day. On a team where responsibilites are more evenly divided, there is a greater chance of getting into the flow and having the greatest day in the world.

## DEVELOPING AND HANDLING THE STAR

No matter how team-oriented we want our group to be and no matter how much we talk about shared responsibility, successful teams develop stars. There will always be people who make a disproportionate contribution to the success of the whole and who get a disproportionate amount of attention. Equal responsibility never means equal performance; it means responsibility to develop one's skill and try one's hardest.

We are hooked on stars. The media focuses on individuals, not groups. Rewards are given to the individual. Stars get all of the recognition, while their teammates stand in the background, out of the camera range. In sports teams, especially, we see one person profit and one person shine as a result, in part, of the total effort—of teamwork and the support of teammates.

Realistically, in any organization, you must find and develop those uniquely talented people who can, in fact, make the big play and put you over the top. Having a star is good. Being a star is a most difficult role for anyone to play, particularly the young, possibly immature athlete. The star must be given the opportunity to shine, yet, the group must be able to identify with him. Praise for him should be praise for everybody.

The way organizations recognize their stars requires skill. Jealousy over who gets what share of the spoils or attention can be a major factor in the breakup of successful organizations. Here prevention is better than the cure. From the beginning, make sure that the team recognizes the reality that, if we succeed, stars will emerge. We want that. It is critical that these stars earn the role they enjoy. These stars cannot be undeserving, created by promotion or propaganda. It is crucial that the star be worthy of the recognition.

*The most important measure of how good a game I played was how much better I'd made my teammates play.*

—Bill Russell

Organizations must prepare emerging stars in advance for their responsibility to the team. The star has to learn how to shine. It is important when mantle falls on him that the star realizes he is a representative of the team. He must promote team values and acknowledge his teammates' contributions. He must use his moment in the spotlight to represent the team as well as himself.

Too often in our society, we have created stars whose only purpose, it seems, is to promote themselves. It takes balance to handle the kind of attention a Michael Jordan or a Joe Montana receives. I have great admiration for both of these men because they use the glare of individual media attention to project an understanding of the team concept.

If you begin to talk about those expectations after the person has been singled out from his peers, ego may get in the way of the message. Knowing his responsibility to others before it happens gives the star a better chance to handle it well.

The USC player learns that he does not do anything to promote himself. We do not allow "dancing" after a play. There are no extra decorations on our uniforms.

*We do not even put names on the uniforms—*
*you can find those in the program*
*if you want. Out on the field*
*every player is a **team** player.*

When you put on the USC uniform, you wear it the same way everybody else does. Off the field we do not try to dominate a player's life, but on the field, as a representative of the team, he is a team member—that is his identity.

## PROBLEM PERFORMERS

The flip side of stardom is problem performers. Coaches must also deal with them. You must quickly identify the performance that cannot continue, the performance that must change, and the consequences of its not changing. When you see a behavior or attitude that cannot continue, it must be made very clear. I am not talking about blame or about threats. It is about what level of performance is a requirement. And it is about finding solutions. No one wants to look bad, and everyone wants to be successful.

When dealing with someone who is causing problems or for whom things are out of sync, the important thing is to try to view the situation from a different perspective. Sometimes we misunderstand people because we are angry with them. I have been in situations where the more I think about someone, the more annoyed I become. I think, "Tomorrow, the first thing he does bad, I'm going to say 'Listen, you....'" Then he'll say, "...", when I walk in and the kid says "Hi," I respond, "Well, let me tell you...."I'm guilty of a negative visualization!

We have all done it! Playing out those destructive scenarios makes them a reality, which is disastrous.

It is hard to catch yourself and to stop looking at problems from a negative frame of mind. Instead, we have to mentally walk behind a person's shoulder and see ourselves and the rest of the team from his viewpoint. That helps answer questions such as "Where is he?" "Is he afraid?" "Is this an uncomfortable environment?" Doing this takes effort, but it allows you to deal with the problem positively. I think we have to do this in most cases if we want a solution.

Take the approach of here is what we're trying to do and here is the problem, then ask people to own the problem and be involved in solving it. Get people to stop being defensive about problems. The issue is not blame, it is finding solutions that improve our performance. Get people involved in considering alternatives. Allow them to arrive at the solution. This is a learning process for both the performers and the coaches. Involvement increases everyone's commitment to doing it right.

## TEAM ETHIC

For an organization to become great, there has to be the capacity to improve constantly, to learn both from defeats and from what we do well. It is easy in the emotion of the moment to say, "We're going to win them all," but that may be foolish for the overall health of your team. What you *must* do, is constantly strive to reinforce your vision. We do that by adhering to a code such as the one we have defined for our defense:

1. Be prepared
2. Play hard
3. Play at maximum speed
4. Finish every play

## WEST POINT HONOR CODE

A cadet will not lie, cheat, or steal nor tolerate those who do.

## THE LEGIONNAIRE'S CODE OF HONOUR

1. Legionnaire: you are a volonteer [sic] serving France faithfully and with honour.

2. Every Legionnaire is your brother-at-arms, irrespective of his nationality, race or creed. You will demonstrate this by an unwavering and straight-forward solidarity which must always bind together members of the same family.

3. Respectful of the Legion's traditions, honouring your superiors, discipline and cameradery are your strength, courage and loyalty your virtues.

4. Proud of your status as that of a legionnaire, you will display this pride by your turnout, always impeccable, your behavior, ever worthy, though modest, your living-quarters, always tidy.

5. An elite soldier: you will train vigorously, you will maintain your weapon as if it were your most precious possession, you will keep your body in the peak of condition, always fit.

6. A mission once given to you becomes sacred to you, you will accomplish it to the end and at all cost.

7. In combat: you will act without relish of your task, or hatred; you will respect the vanquished enemy and will never abandon neither your wounded nor your dead, nor will you under any circumstances surrender your arms.

*Source: Commandement de la Légion Etrangère*

That code may seem deceptively simple, but it captures the essence of how we want to constantly improve performance. I got the notion of a code from the movie, *A Few Good Men.* "We are the Marines, we have a code—unit, corps, God, country," that type of thing. As the leader you determine what the code is. Solicit input from the team and from your fellow coaches.

The initial step is determining what constitutes excellence that you can control and measure. Preparation is a key for our performance, so we work with the group to define what "prepared" is. We ask every player to tell us what prepared is, what playing hard is. This gives us a way of analyzing and debriefing a performance.

Our code helps us review and analyze our performance as a way to constantly improve. Most of us could list on one hand the number of times we tried our very hardest. While we might say, "I tried as hard as I could," we honestly rarely do give our heart and soul. In football, the person who becomes really involved begins to be curious about just how hard he could play. If his version of "playing hard" is not good enough, we can deal with the level of conditioning. Maybe he got tired; we can improve his stamina.

We can evaluate and measure being prepared. For a salesman, "being prepared" might mean that he is going to have a prospectus and an analysis of the customer every single time he makes a sales call. You can make an appointment, be on time, look presentable. There are things that you can evaluate and control. You can identify and do the things that mean being prepared in your environment.

We spend a lot of time coaching maximum speed. If you run a 40-yard dash in 4.7 seconds, there is not much you can do to improve. But in football, speed is related to changing direction. There is an opportunity to be inefficient in what we call fishhooks. We spend a lot of time teaching abrupt, tight, straight-angle turns, which redirect without wasting time. This ability to change direction quickly can increase playing speed. So can learning to get up quickly after a fall. We can analyze speed and train these types of improvements.

### EXAMPLES AS MODELS

We use examples and stories to help people understand our code and what being prepared and trying hard means. We are a football team with a proud tradition, so we constantly try to build on that and to reinforce in the player's mind our image of how a USC team member prepares and plays. We do that in several ways. I talk about the chemistry of past seasons. What I try to describe is the process of how we achieve great wins. I talk about people like Ronnie Lott—not just his great plays, but Ronnie Lott on the practice field, his energy, the look in his eye, the kind of a fierceness that he had about almost everything he did, the example he was, almost like he was on fire. You looked at Ronnie and you almost expected to see smoke coming out of his ears on a normal practice day. Ronnie retained that fervor throughout his career. He is considered one of the most determined, fiercest, and most fanatical players in mod-

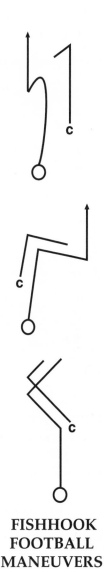

**FISHHOOK FOOTBALL MANEUVERS**

USC Sports Information
*Ronnie Lott*

$A$s we research [ed]... excellent companies, we were struck by the dominant use of story, slogan, and legend as people tried to explain the characteristics of their own great institutions....these stories, myths, and legends appear to be very important, because they convey the organization's shared values, or culture.[1]

ern football. He has a passion for the game that burns on almost a daily basis. That is who he was. Certainly, he ranks high in comparison with others who have played the game.

In using him as a standard for us, the Ronnie Lott that I try to bring alive is not just the guy being carried of the field or holding a trophy, to my people he is the guy who was willing to do the extra things and who demanded the same from his friends and teammates.

I tell my team right away about any example of how present stars prepare. As coaches, we try to give examples of present sports greats in terms of what the star is willing to do to get ready. If our player prepares at a "B" or "C" level, the great athlete prepares at an "A+" level. And that superstar is gifted! It is ridiculous for our players not to prepare at an "A+" level. If they have hopes or dreams of being anything like their heroes, they have to prepare intensely. I think those kind of stories are really important to building the ethic I want my players to have about the process: preparing and coming armed with a sense of the preparation. Young people sometimes mistake their idols' showmanship for the substance they should aim to duplicate. Competition and the media skew our idea of greatness. They expose us to the person at the moment of glory. We see the tip of the iceberg. We do not see below the surface of a great performance. People who focus on the event have little understanding of the preparation behind it.

There is a great story that I heard secondhand about the Olympic "Dream Team" that included Magic Johnson and Michael Jordan. They were beating their opponents by wide margins, and in this particular example, they were preparing to play a less-than-challenging opponent. The pregame locker room was filled with Olympics people, sponsors, and so forth. There was a party atmosphere. People were signing autographs.

Nobody could find Michael Jordan. They eventually found him in a back room studying a videotape of the player that he was going to play opposite. The player was not anywhere near Michael's caliber, and everybody knew that, but Michael Jordan, the greatest basketball player on earth, was not going out there unprepared. I think you have to build that ethic into your group. If I am prepared, I will succeed. If I am not, I do not feel right. I want my team to have a hunger for preparation, otherwise they don't possess the energy necessary to succeed in competition. Building that takes a lot of work. That is where a lot of our coaching and leadership energy goes.

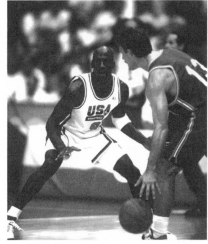

*Focus On Sports*

*Michael Jordan*

I also use examples of how senior members of the team developed. As an example, a senior who becomes an NFL first-round draft choice will get a Mercedes when he signs his contract. He earned this because of the tremendous effort he made in conditioning last year between spring training and training camp. In holding him up as an example, I ask the player to close his eyes and drive his clunker car up beside this Mercedes and to visualize both of them. Then I tell him, "You're a clunker now, but you're going to be a Mercedes." Every time I catch him making an effort, I tell him, "You just earned yourself a Mercedes' rear-view mirror, or a tailpipe, or whatever." I hope there are thousands of parts on that car! Now it is a game we play. When he puts out a great effort he will say to me, "Coach, what was that worth?" He is learning to try his hardest, and the learning is fun!

## TEAM LEADERSHIP

Leadership on a team is dynamic. Structuring it too much seems to inhibit the contributions that others can

## Lessons from Geese*
—by Milton Olson

1. As each bird flaps its wings, it creates an "uplift" for the bird following. By flying in a "V" formation, the whole flock adds 71% greater flying range than if the bird flew alone.

*Lesson: People who share a common direction and sense of community can get where they are going more quickly and easily because they are traveling on the thrust of one another.*

2. Whenever a goose falls out of formation, it suddenly feels the drag and resistance of trying to fly alone, and it quickly gets back into formation to take advantage of the "lifting power" of the bird immediately in front.

*Lesson: If we have as much sense as a goose, we will stay in formation with those who are headed where we want to go (and be willing to accept their help as well as give ours to the others).*

3. When the lead goose gets tired, it rotates back into the formation and another goose flies at the point position.

*Lesson: It pays to take turns doing the hard tasks, and sharing leadership—with people, as with geese, we are interdependent with one another.*

4. The geese in formation honk from behind to encourage those up front to keep up their speed.

*Lesson: We need to make sure our honking from behind is encouraging—and not something else.*

5. When a goose gets sick or wounded or shot down, two geese drop out of formation and follow it down to help and protect it. They stay with it until it is able to fly again or dies. Then they launch out on their own, with another formation, or catch-up with the flock.

*Lesson: If we have as much sense as geese we, too, will stand by one another in difficult times as well as when we are strong.*

---

*This story was supplied courtesy of Three Dog Down, Polson, Montana. The original publisher is unknown.

make. Teams that designate someone as the leader create a wait-and-see attitude ("Let George do it") in everyone else. The best leadership emerges from the team and is a natural response to the situations that present themselves. Such leaders are fostered by the team. The team, rather than the coach, gives this person permission to lead.

Leadership within a team—the spontaneous kind—is often passed back and forth. Team leadership is practiced in many small ways. One individual encourages another; one group motivates an other group. This leadership adds enthusiasm and determination to teams from the inside. It is not something that a coach can designate. Good teams display this kind of leadership.

## SUMMARY

Individualism versus conformity is the new standard and it is demanding fundamental changes in the managers' communication and organizational development skills. The challenge, whether it occurs in the locker room or in the board room, is to train players to think as a unit while simultaneously ensuring that each individual gives his personal best. The most successful teams are the ones that have done the most to develop their people and to create the greatest sense of belonging. To succeed you need a goal, a game plan or system for successful team management, and a way to gauge commitment—both by the organization to its people and vice versa.

*A* college football team turns over personnel faster than any other organization. We are allowed a total of 85 players. We graduate and recruit 20 to 25 new men each year. So 20 to 25 percent of our organization is new each year. Players' selection, recruitment, and integration into the organization is our life's blood.

# SELECTING
# YOUR TEAM

*I'm not hiring for where I am;*
*I'm hiring for where I'll be.*

Fred Bramante, Jr.

*We don't start out with the assumption*
*our company is for everybody.*

William G. McGowan

# 5

## BE INVOLVED

Each member of an organization is an extension of the leader. As an organization's cast changes, there must be a little piece of the leader and of the leader's vision in every new hire. The process of selecting people is too important to delegate. The people you recruit are the organization's future. If you delegate that selection process to your managers or to Human Resources, *look out*. The result may be an organization that you do not recognize, and it can happen in a very short period of time.

In addition to guiding the organization's future, your involvement in the recruiting process also maximizes the new hire's chance of success. When I see and approve of each new member, I become invested in his future with the organization. My sense of involvement and caring for people that I had a stake in selecting is much greater. It is not a matter of not trusting the judgment of others or of disapproving of their selection. The issue is whether or not a connection is there.

A significant aspect of the recruitment and selection process is giving the candidate an opportunity to select you. The candidate does not yet know what your organization stands for, what the job involves, or what is expected of members.

*Through the selection process,*
*you want to foster a desire*
*to become a part of your team*
*and enthusiasm for building your vision.*

This may be even more important than establishing that a candidate has the potential and the skills that you are looking for, which you can verify in many ways outside of personal interviews.

Some leaders find it impossible to be involved in the selection of everyone. Their organizations are too big or are growing too fast. In these situations, the team of people involved in the selection process must be imbued with the importance of the task. Guiding this group is crucial. That means working with them to establish the criteria for selection. And in these organizations, the leader must be personally involved in the recruitment of *key* positions.

Establish criteria as a group; otherwise each assistant coach will establish his own. By working together to agree on criteria and measurements of both the tangibles and the intangibles, there is a shared vision of the required talent. Teamwork in the recruiting process helps people resist the temptation to select someone with all of the intangibles, all of the behavioral traits. A candidate may possess the discipline, the courage, and the emotion to do the job but still be lacking in required characteristics, which for football might be physical attributes such as weight or height.

When managers and coaches are involved in deciding the criteria and in selecting the new team members, they are more invested in their success, in developing that team member. The coach builds on that investment and cooperation with the other members of the coaching staff. An assistant coach who has not participated in either the selection criteria or the evaluation of new people may not fully sign off on someone. If he is not fully invested in this person's success, he is more judgmental: "*I'll* decide whether you can really do it or not."

## ESTABLISH CRITERIA

Whether the organization is large or small, whether the leader is fully involved in the selection process or just guiding it, he has to establish criteria. The vision for the organization dictates that. Different talents and skills are required for different roles. If you are hiring someone for a particular role in a functional area of the organization, define what the job is and what it takes to do it given where this organization is heading. How critical is it to your organization to be the best in service or technological skills? Does the job require someone who really enjoys working with people, someone who is a good problem solver, or someone with a detail orientation? All of these affect job requirements. It colors the picture of who would fit what role.

The organization's capabilities also dictate some criteria. If I say, "I see something here and I believe that this person can be developed," I had better possess both a developmental plan and the skill to effect it. You may

Focus On Sports

*Julius Erving, "Dr. J.," was considered tall at 6'6" in the late 70s.*

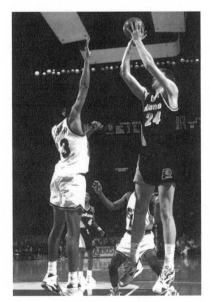

Focus On Sports

*Rik Smits at 7'4" is tall by today's standards.*

decide that you want people with certain characteristics—outgoing, well-organized, well-educated—and you will teach them job-specific skills. Avoid overestimating your ability to train. Coaches think, "It's okay. We'll train him." Sometimes we deceive ourselves and think that we can overcome any obstacle to develop missing skills to make someone fit our organization. This is not true. We often make this mistake when an extremely talented player has played a position for a while. We get confused and credit the player's success to our coaching. But the player's replacement may present a different set of challenges, and we may not have the coaching skills to deal with them. Don't overestimate your teaching contribution; I have done it.

If your organization is not set up to train people, you must define the skills and the experiences the person should have, as well as the characteristics. You may need a salesperson who has already demonstrated that he can sell. Obviously, you still have to train him about your own product, but you have a running start.

We have to constantly revisit our criteria because they are constantly shifting. For us, the changes are subtle. Someone's image of a quarterback or an offensive lineman may become obsolete. Where an offensive tackle five years ago might have been 6'3" and 240 pounds, now you may need someone who is 6'6" and 290 pounds. Years ago 6'6" was considered tall for a basketball player; today's "giants" tower at 7'6". As a business or technology matures, their requirements change in the same way.

When the leader cannot be fully involved

in the selection process, it is important that there be some sort of introduction or ritualistic process through which new members meet and talk to the leader, or at least hear his vision for the organization. Some leaders of large organizations send each new hire a personal letter of welcome, do personal introductions of new hires in the organization's newsletter or on e-mail, or arrange orientation lunch meetings.

## LOOK FOR TALENT!

When asked what he looked for in recruiting players, John Wooden, UCLA's great former basketball coach, used to say, "Talent, talent, talent." The first requirement is talent. That is what we try to define. Morale, spirit, and teamwork will not win for us without talent. Talent is what gives us a chance to win; without talent, we have no chance. Without the necessary talent, if we are playing a superior opponent, we will lose no matter how spirited and emotional we are.

*The right attributes married to desire will always win over desire trying to overcome a lack of attributes.*

To be a champion organization, the first requirement is talent followed by the refinement of that talent into the right skills—skills that work—and the right habits. An organization wants to attract the best people with the right skills and talents. The right skills are the ones that support and forward the organization's vision and strategies.

The coach or manager who does not recognize talent, who cannot look at a player and see his potential, is doomed to deal with average players. Plenty of people overcompensate for and overcome physical obstacles to become successful. "Here is Joe, he was not the biggest or the best, but he did it!" Courage and determination are important criteria, but if you are not careful, pretty soon you have got eight Joes. You have fallen victim to using the exception as your criterion because you admire the person's accomplishments so much. However, it is still better to recruit the person with the desire *and* the characteristics to be the best. The right attributes married to desire will always win over desire trying to overcome a lack of attributes.

## RESIST MEDIOCRITY

Often an organization's culture promotes recruiting mediocrity because it is safe; the recruit fits codes or core models, but he is an average talent. In looking for the perfect package, it is easy to be seduced by the safe one. Spotting talent is harder than you might expect. A common pitfall is to judge players by the standards of another generation. The person who does the talent scouting may focus on someone who displays a work ethic that he can relate to. It is understandable for a scout to judge superficial discipline and mistake it for talent. There is a temptation to select people with moderate amounts of skills A, B, and C if we think that they will not cause problems, they will behave well and follow the rules, and they will be comfortable for us to coach. That is the quickest path to a pretty average team of all-around average guys. No coach can take a person without talent or a person with average talent and make him great. That is why it is important to select the person who has phenomenal skills in at least one area.

A recruiter may also overlook potential or talent when it is hidden in a package that he does not appreciate—a young player's weird clothing or hairstyle. These are of no significance. In selecting someone who he is going to work with, an assistant coach or manager may unconsciously opt for someone who is easy to coach, who gives his all, and who does not have eccentric qualities. Companies often judge applicants by their dress or their speech. Those things may be important, very important, but they are not the essential talent. Those things are teachable. Talent is not. Some coaches who are "discipline coaches" want discipline or attitude more than they want the talent. The important thing is the person's talent and enthusiasm for the game (or the organization's vision); if he has that, we want him.

*I*s there something here we can hang our hat on? Is there one thing he can do?

—Al Davis

## DON'T EXPECT A COMPLETE PACKAGE

Talent does not come in complete packages. One of Al Davis' chief sayings was "Is there something here we can hang our hat on? Is there one thing he can do?" If there was, the Raiders would go after that player and then work to develop him. No coach can take a person without talent or a person with average talent and make him great. Talent and love for the game can yield a great player. In our environment, we have to have great players. We must see beyond peripherals to the essential talent and invite only the best to join us—in whatever shape that happens to present itself!

© *Joel Zwink/NFL Photos*

*Al Davis, owner and managing general partner of the Oakland Raiders.*

The Raiders' pursuit of talent was the basis for their willingness to accept diversity and individuality in the Al Davis-John Madden-Tom Flores period. The Raiders looked for talented players who had trouble getting along in other organizations. If a guy was a big talent, but was disruptive, the Raiders would grab him up. When they brought him in, they told him that all they cared about was that he played hard and was a good team member. It did not matter what he did outside the team, if he was crazy, rode a motorcycle, shaved his head, whatever. They put up with the player's idiosyncrasies as long as he gave his best effort. But if he did not play hard, then he was out of there. That philosophy appealed to a certain kind of person who did not want to

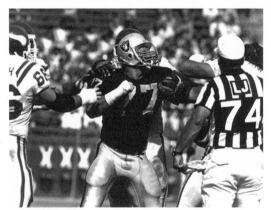

© *Jim Chaffin/NFL Photos*

*The Raiders earned a reputation for being the "bad" boys of the NFL. Lyle Alzado in action.*

feel harassed by rules and who felt "these people understand me." The Raiders seduced these guys into conforming where it was important.

As a coach we would love to find someone who is great at everything. That rarely happens. When a coach finds someone with the potential for greatness in him, he must help the person develop. I admired John Madden's ability to be really comfortable working with people on the Raiders who were all over the map. He could almost snap his fingers and say, "Okay, it's time for business" and that diverse group would go right to work. They had that ethic. When business was over, it was another story.

## TAKE RISKS

Your organization has to support risk-taking when looking for great talent. If you find talent in some type of incomplete package, you are always taking a risk that you will be able to develop it. A talented individual who ignores his responsibility to be a team member presents us with the challenge of coaching him in teamwork. This leaves us a little more at risk as coaches. But the payback is worth it if we can develop those skills; we have a championship player. Companies face the same risk; they may have to compensate for or develop specific aspects of great talents—the communication skills of the technological genius, the financial expertise of the talented manager, or the organizational skills of the great salesperson.

College recruiters tend to shy away from young athletes from the inner city because of the perceived risk.

The deprivation and problems of inner city life are so overwhelming—increased use of violent weapons, the prevalence of drug cultures, family structures and schools that have deteriorated—that it is difficult to survive. What these young people experience can cause them to bring a lot of "baggage" with them. So people are tempted to back away from them. It is natural to think, "I don't need that. I'll find more acceptable risks and easier to coach talent."

At USC, we believe that it is very important to thoroughly investigate the young athletes in the inner city. Many are extremely talented and have great motivation to succeed. Whatever the risks, they are well worth taking. A kid who comes from a less-than-ideal environment but who also possesses a lot of talent, ambition, and a real love of the game can be very successful. We may have to deal with someone with a street ethic. All of us have multiple roles, but certainly one of them must be taking risks to develop talent that might otherwise be lost to all of us.

## OUR KIND OF GUY

Think about how a person will fit into your organization. Even when you have found a very talented individual who you want to join your organization, it is not a foregone conclusion that he will fit in and be happy. If he comes from a farm in Kansas, life in a big city may be uncomfortable. Will someone from New York City be able to settle into a small town in Indiana? Someone who grew up in California may hate New England winters. Someone who is very homesick, who hates life on our campus, our weather, or our traffic is ultimately going to be defeated.

Think about the cultural fit, too. When we ask if someone is "a USC kind of guy" we are trying to decide if he will fit in here and with the team. Will this person

**L**ife As a Trojan Athlete...

♦ **Play one of the nation's toughest schedules**

♦ **Play before sellout crowds in historic Los Angeles Memeorial Coliseum**

♦ **Be interviewed by the country's second-largest media contingent**

♦ **Be seen on national or regional television every week**

♦ **Wear the Cardinal & Gold uniform of USC** [1]

enjoy going to school here? Each organization has its own culture, and the new person has to fit that style or be able to adapt to it. In the selection process, we ask the candidate to evaluate this. We expose him to the different aspects of our organization and have him talk to some of our experienced people. The person has to be comfortable with "how we do things here."

Our kind of guy is a "gym rat" who likes to hang around athletic venues. That is where he is comfortable. He enjoys being with his team. These are not kids with a wide range of interests. They are not into a lot of different things. Remember, we are not looking for the generalist—the well-balanced, well-rounded person. Often the generalist is not that desirable. A USC kind of guy might not fit into a mold that well. He is comfortable with people who are different from himself. He does not take himself too seriously, though we want him to be passionately attached to his talent and the game. More than anything, we want people who love to play; the Bonnie Blairs of football. And they have to be willing to give what it takes to be the best that they can be.

Some people say that I recruit guys who are not perfect gentleman, who have been in trouble in the past, who perhaps look less than well-groomed. I have to be able to respond with confidence, "Yes, but these people have something special to offer. At the core of their beings are people who have got greatness in them." If someone has screwed up in some areas, we are willing to help them with problems in that area while we take advantage of their core greatness. We believe we can teach them how to become a Trojan. This is what we must constantly address ourselves to—helping people grow within the organization.

# INDIVIDUAL COMMITMENT, NOT CONFORMITY

Competence is the first responsibility that players take on when they join any team. They bring a level of competence to the organization, and they take on the responsibility to improve that competence. Often that sense of responsibility to the group is tested when it comes to improving one's skills.

The individual should feel that he has something to contribute. That motivation can drive his efforts: "This group needs me." This provides a perfect opportunity for the head coach in recruiting new members. The coach can describe the organization's vision, what the prospective player can contribute, and what is expected of him. If a new employee says, "I didn't expect it to be like this" or "That's not what you told me," an opportunity has been missed to build understanding and commitment.

A company cannot ask team members to commit everything, but in the commitment to important team responsibilities, we will not compromise. They have to learn about team play and about how hard we prepare. If they do not learn to prepare or to be a team member, they cannot stay here.

This is a very important part of any commitment you get from and give to your people. They have the chance to do some of what they want on their time. Personal hobbies are their own business. They understand that you are not asking for them to be company people all the time. But, in return, you want commitment to your ethic. Good teams tend to encourage a certain kind of conformity to that ethic. They let members know how to behave: "We don't do that here." If someone wears weird clothes, they might comment on it, but there is a space between commenting and condemning. On our team you can be weird and you can do what you want, as long as you are fully committed to us.

There is a big difference between this generation and my generation in the area of individuality and conformity. In my day you showed that you had committed yourself to a team or an organization by modeling yourself after them. You drove their kind of car. You wore their kind of clothes. An organization that wants to become the best must avoid people who are too willing to be "company people," who are looking for a secure little nest where they can play it safe. With the alternative, you may have to listen to discordant voices, but your organization will be better for it.

However, in the final analysis, the crux of the issue is neither conformity nor diversity—it is commitment. You can come in here as long as you commit yourself to the team effort. Our yardstick is what the team member is willing to do to further the vision, mission, and the code of our group.

## SUMMARY

Selection is a two-way street. It is as much a process of the candidates selecting you and your organization as it is of you selecting them. This is very important. Selection is more about asking recruits to make a choice of your team than it is about you verifying that they are competent. You want people who want to work for your organization.

The recruit will learn how to become one of us because we will teach him. We must constantly focus on helping this person grow within the organization. The new team member must take pride in developing and in continuing to grow. No one ever plateaus or reaches the limit of his potential. Skills must be practiced every day to become and stay sharp and to grow.

*Great teams, teams that make things happen, are teams that develop great skill in every function. The burden winning is shared equally. The entire team wins and the entire team loses. Their identity as team members inspires responsibility. They share an energy and a joy in working together. They are dedicated to the ongoing process of mastering new levels of skill and endurance. Losses are a painful learning ground, winning a spur to new challenges, Making this happen is what every coach strives for.*

# Making It Happen

*I call systems thinking the fifth discipline because it is...a shift of mind from seeing parts to seeing wholes, from seeing people as helpless reactors to seeing them as active participants in shaping their reality, from reacting to the present to creating the future...[it] is the cornerstone of how learning organizations think around their world.*

Peter Senge, *The Fifth Discipline*

# 6

## Phases of Growth

There are two phases in "Making it Happen":

1. "Building the Engine"
2. "Keeping It Running"

The start-up, turnaround, and reinvention of an organization—all the new beginnings—demand everything you have got. You must be an absolute dynamo to get an organization going on a new path. If you are the leader, this takes total commitment to making things happen. Everyone feeds off your energy. They look to you for

*USC Sports Information*

*Coach Robinson demonstrates to USC players how it is done.*

answers. As the leader you must create the vision and exemplify commitment to it. To set that example, you must pay attention to every detail. every other phase of your life must simply be put on hold.

But this cannot go on forever. You cannot keep that pace up. Nor should it remain at that level once the organization is operational. When you have had some success, when things are starting to take shape and are beginning to move smoothly in the direction you want, transition into phase two, "Keeping It Running."

The second phase, keeping the organization running and tuned up, is different from the first one and requires different things from you. Once the organization is moving in harmony, you must be willing to pull back to allow others to become involved.

When you are changing direction and keeping it running, your every day, ongoing example establishes the ethic and the culture and reinforces these core values. It answers everyone's questions about what the organization stands for and how to act. You must also talk about and exemplify the ethic, but it is how you act and what you do every day rather than what you say that defines the ethic you teach.

## BUILDING THE ENGINE

To make a new beginning, you have to make changes on every front at the same time. You have to be everywhere, breathing energy and life into every phase of the organization. You are, in fact, the spark plug for everything that is going on. This is when there is not a lot of time for sleep or thoughts other than "Making It Happen." This is always the best of times for me.

During the start-up phase, you are everything to this organization. You are involved in everything. It is your baby. You are quite directive. But letting go and letting the organization grow up starts very quickly. Allowing others to control and nurture your baby can be difficult. Every parent who raises a child experiences this. They know that backing off—starting when they drop their child off at nursery school—is a very gradual process (over fifteen years in the case of children). It is gradual; it cannot be sudden. You gradually relinquish ownership by sharing part of your initial role.

You gave it your all and the organization is rolling along. It embodies everything that you believe. You can see the dreams coming true. Everything is moving forward as it should be. What do you do now? You must transition from total control to sharing and adjusting your role. This is difficult, and the right balance is obscure at times. It can be difficult on your ego. It does not happen at once. It evolves.

## KEEPING IT RUNNING

The transition into phase two is a gradual one; a shift from "mine" to "ours." You can make a big mistake if you keep going—from "ours" to "theirs." That is overdelegating.

In phase two, assistant coaches still respect the need to check with you. They still need your direction. Provide guidance but avoid stifling their initiative. Encourage them to take initiative. Begin to let other people take over in certain areas. Gradually let them drive the building of the shared vision.

©Richard Mackson/NFL Photos

*John Robinson confers with a member of his Rams' coaching staff.*

The coaching staff you hire must include people who will actively seek to take your responsibility away from you at the appropriate time. Initially, they are willing to further your vision, but eventually they become invested in the vision and want their percentage of responsibility to increase. Your vision is now being expressed through this coaching team. They are an extension of you, not a new direction. Constantly verify that. Needing to do so is a good problem.

*Dealing with a competitive, creatively involved staff is better than dealing with people who need your energy and decision making to function.*

Once you hit cruise control on the operation, you must develop more curiosity about what is going on outside the organization. What are the new ideas? What are other teams doing? Replace immersion in the day-to-day details with taking stock of the need to change or correct course. Use your network of friends and other leaders to gather data. Use this opportunity to go out and seek new ideas. While your managers are totally involved in the process, you are giving up immersion in the details and starting to invigorate the operation with new ideas, new thoughts.

Balance this with finding a way to keep up with changes taking place in your own organization. Encourage assistant coaches to use you as a sounding board. Devote a certain amount of time to review what is going on. I have people put together papers and edited videos together so that I can keep in touch without the full investment of time that it would take if I reviewed everything myself.

There have been three instances of new beginnings in my career. I have concluded that I know how to do the first part very well. I know how to invigorate it. I know how to get an organization moving fast in the direction that I want. I have had mixed results with the second phase. At times I have overmanaged and at other times overdelegated—then lost interest, and secretly got bored. At these times, I have subconsciously been looking around for a new challenge. So I am still learning; I face a challenge in learning how to improve my role in keeping it running.

## THE TEAM ETHIC

We must define our values and code, then communicate them with everyone: respect for people and the game, trying our hardest, being prepared. Actions must demonstrate that we are all in this together. No one is exempt. Everyone must see core values in what you do; for example, you are the first one there, you are prepared for meetings.

### INTEGRITY

We reinforce the integrity of the game through respect for the rules. Behind those rules is the principle of fairness, of equal advantage. The game deserves respect. The notion that it is okay to win at any cost is not praiseworthy—despite what popular culture may seem to indicate. We must shun that. Ignoring the rules and doing whatever it takes to achieve selfish, personal gain is destructive for society, for business, and for the game.

Coach everyone in their responsibility to protect the integrity of the game, to act fairly, for example, to not spy on opponents or seek inside information. If someone walked into my office and said, "Guess whose practice I saw yesterday and do you know what they are doing?" I must say, without hesitation, "I don't want to know." Guarding against temptation means that we must talk out issues away from the action, to establish clear-cut responses before being confronted with such situations.

**At the NFL knee injury clinic**

Leaving no doubt about the standards we expect requires us to have thought about it and talked about it. We have to train team members how to treat opponents. The thought of doing something that would injure another player is abhorrent. Player's knees are particularly vulnerable. A hit in the knee can lead to surgery and consequences to one's career. We want our players to be careful not to attack an opponent in that area. We know how those injuries happen. We have to discuss with players how to tackle the opponent as hard as they can in a legitimate fashion, instilling in them that they win by playing fair, and by being better. We stress that you demean yourself if you do not respect your opponent. We win by physically dominating the game so that the opponent gives in. We must be a force that can intimidate the opponent by who we are. And we do that ethically. We tell our players that being tough is in the eyes, not in the mouth. It is never a pretense. When someone accomplishes success within a set of rules, there is a sense of achievement.

*W*arren Bennis' definition of the difference between a manager and a leader—one does things right and the other does the right thing

## Your Key Executives

Your coaches are the key to succeeding in both of these phases. The best assistant coaches in the early phase are people who are willing to do what I ask them to do and who take it to the end. When you are making a new beginning, the coaching team must be willing to enthusiastically execute your vision. But you also want them to want to increase their percentage of influence over time. It is crucial to get the right people in the first phase who will not short-circuit when they must take more initiative in the second phase.

This reminds me of Warren Bennis' definition of the difference between a manager and a leader—one does things right and the other does the right thing. If you simply recruit managers, you will never move beyond the first phase. Look for leaders who are willing to be part of a team but who want to grow and ultimately have your job. As the head coach, you must develop a pact with this select group that you will give them opportunities to grow and to move on; you will help them find better jobs or the right job when the right time comes.

It is a mistake in hiring your coaches to try to control them, to keep them in the box where they already do a good job, and not to allow them to develop new skills. They may want to leave you when that growth occurs. That is okay! You want your best people to constantly think about leaving you. When their expertise has improved, they are ready to move on. When it is time for them to leave the nest, help put air under their wings. This is the pact you make with them. Do not try to keep good people indefinitely. You keep them for a period of time. When they outgrow their job, either promote them—maybe you can move over a bit and make them a partner—or help them find a better job somewhere else. If someone comes to you with growth in mind and it does not happen, he begins to malfunction. He suffers from the same thing you might be suffering from; he loses interest.

Your key executives are temporary. Provide the best possible environment for them; share your vision and the creativity of building something new, and give them an opportunity to grow. This provides kind of security because, if they are fulfilled in their jobs, motivated, and

*The team must care about and respect the team as well as individual members. That is part of the ethic you establish as a leader*

confident about their future, they are not going to jump at the first opportunity that comes their way. You want them to be happy here and not to feel stifled or stunted working with you. The cage is not locked, and they do not feel trapped. They are only going to leave you for the perfect, the right job. That is the security of loyalty that is freely given.

## YOUR TEAM

The basic premise of any team is that together we can do a lot more than any of us can accomplish separately. More than that, the individuals on the team personally can accomplish a lot more in a team setting than they could on their own.

The team and the individuals are not going to succeed unless they find a commonality, unless the effort of the group's work becomes more important than the goals of the individuals.

*Everybody must be convinced that it will be more rewarding to work for the team versus individual goals.*

In our society, people are willing to commit to a group if they can maintain some of their individuality and if they believe that the team is willing to work for them if they work for the team. The team must care about and respect the team as well as individual members. That is part of the ethic you establish as a leader. When most of us look back, we see that some of our most rewarding experiences are those we shared with others, when we were part of a cause, when we did it together.

## DEMONSTRATE BELONGING

Wanting to belong is natural. The person who comes into an organization wants more than anything else to be accepted by the team members. He thinks, "Boy, I hope everybody likes me. I hope I'm okay with these people," not "I'm here to establish my point of view." Even the nonconformist wants to be accepted. As we grow older we belong to fewer groups and our range of friends narrows. Making the workplace a team can fulfill our need to do important work and to belong.

UPI/Bettmann

*The Oakland A's celebrate their victory over the Giants in the fourth and final game of the 1989 World Series.*

Developing the team needs daily attention. It requires symbols that reinforce that you are part of the team—hats, T-shirts, team photographs. Reinforce the team concept by creating a work atmosphere that is conducive to success. Provide training and educational opportunities. Pay attention to the physical plant. Emphasize employee health and safety. Stay attuned to personal needs that team members might have, such as flexible time to provide child or elder care. Demonstrate respectful, attentive, and friendly behavior toward colleagues. All of these reinforce the team concept.

All of this creates a sense that the organization cares about the team, that you are special because you are on this team. Demonstrate that caring in whatever ways work in your organization. Always look for ways to unify this group. The point is that it does not matter what your role is, you are special because you are here.

## DEMAND IMPROVEMENT

The team must be challenged. You must ask them constantly to improve. The quest to be better is the most exciting time. Challenge your team and constantly set specific goals for improvement—improve in these ways, improve these skills. Let them know "We're working for you. We have enhanced your work environment with air-conditioning, noise reduction devices, and flowers. We have provided whatever you need to facilitate improvement." But also let them know why. This is not to create a snug little nest, a comfort zone. We are trying to create the optimum environment for success. We are going to treat you well, but we are also going to ask you to perform. This is a two-way street. The bar must constantly be raised. The team must constantly seek improvement.

When they do perform, reward that. The most conventional reward is a raise; money is always important. Sometimes you cannot afford it. And even when you can, it is never enough. Or you cannot give everyone a raise. So money is not the ideal reward. And people do not just work for money. We can recognize performance in a thousand ways, and we should. Talk about it, post clippings and photos. On a football team this can be fairly emotional. We celebrate the performance, for the individual and for the team. The team won! Our celebrations reinforce our image of ourselves as winners. This is important. As a coach I must be prepared for this moment. When I meet the press, I must take the opportunity to reinforce team values, our sense of what it means to belong to this group, the joy of working together. Our star must also reinforce these same values and acknowledge his teammates and the joy of playing hard, the fact that they want to succeed again.

*You're only as good as your last game, and after today, this game is history.*

—Nolan Richardson,
Coach, Arkansas
Razorbacks

When we win, it is also important to let it go, to leave it behind (just as we do with losses), and to quickly start preparing to win again. No result, winning or losing, is forever. It is another stop on the road to becoming better and better.

## USE LOSSES TO WIN

If you do not meet our collective expectations, we are not going to make you turn in your badge. We have to learn how to fix the problem. The first lesson in accepting a loss is that we all share the defeat. The attitude of "I confess, it was his fault" can do tremendous harm. We all lost. If we lose, we all lose. It is the leader's role to determine what went wrong, where it started to unravel, and how to make that right.

The first thing to acknowledge about losing is that it is painful. And it should always be painful. Every time I have lost a game I am surprised by how much it physically hurts. And that is good. One should never accept too much solace about a loss. Do not seek justification from friends. I do not want people to tell me that we played well, that it was due to the referees, the wind, the rain, or whatever. People will say, "It's okay." No! We lost. It is not okay. We tried our best and we lost. That hurts! Do not allow others to help you make that pain go away. Acknowledge the pain of losing. When you start to plan to win again, that pain begins to subside.

Losing can be very serious for a team. There is the danger that players can become timid after a failure. We all feel this fear when we have made an error. Even fans, when their team loses, do not want to feel that pain any more. They do not want to root as hard again because if it is not important, it will not hurt so much if the team loses. So the response is, "I'm not going to put my heart into it any more, because I don't want my heart broken."

*This is the danger when you allow*
*yourself to wallow in the pain of*
*losing or when you try to blank it out.*
*Either way, you do not learn from it.*

We take on the trappings of losers; our body language and our spirit changes. This will not do! Like the stages of grief, you have to go through it. Otherwise, you are vulnerable to repeating it. Being scared of the possibility of failure is healthy. Accept it and let it build your determination to avoid it again.

Planning to win again starts with accepting the defeat. In acknowledging a loss, quickly analyze what went wrong and reinforce yourself with what went right. Why did we lose?

*In most cases we lost because 10 percent*
*or less of our effort went awry.*
*We did something improperly. So 90 percent*
*or more of our effort was good*
*enough to win.*

In analyzing defeat, the coach needs to point out the specific things that caused the failure, while acknowledging what went well. This way you can plan to eliminate the things that did not work and keep what is good.

In my business, the plan to deal with the loss has to happen fast. By 6:00 PM Sunday, we have to be focused on winning the next game. As coaches we must take the lead. The team starts feeling better and more energized as soon as we start planning for the next game, as soon as we start planning to win again. One of the things that we do is to physically reenact on our practice field what happened, with a different ending. That demonstrates how we might have done it and puts the loss to bed. The players can then acknowledge it; we made these mistakes and to correct them we need to improve these skill areas. If we practice, we will be strong enough to do this. Now we are prepared for the next win.

## COMPETITORS ARE WINNERS

Losses can build determination. There is a steel-like strength that you can get from the loss as soon as you start to plan to win again. One of the common denominators of most great people is that they lost a lot. I am a

Winston Churchill fan; for a while, he lost all the time. Edison tried over 200 variations of the light bulb before he got it to work. Chester Carlson could not get anyone to take the Xerox machine seriously for about twenty years. Great men are shaped by defeat. That is true of teams as well.

*It is wrong to say it does not matter whether you win or lose. It is very important to try to win. But it is also important to see winning as a process of improving over a period of time.*

Our society seems to define winners as whoever wins the game. We have made it so that no matter what level you achieve, if you do not win the ultimate prize, you are almost ridiculed. We seem so vindictive toward anybody that fails—in entertainment, politics, sports, or any aspect of public life—that it discourages people from taking risks. We focus on the one-dimensional image of the winner being congratulated for an outcome and ignore that process that produced the performance. This person is the best because he won. At the same time, the loser is ridiculed, his effort criticized. There are a lot of bad messages there.

Winners deserve congratulations. It is important to compete to win. It is wrong to say it does not matter whether you win or lose. It is very important to try to win. But it is also important to see winning as a process of improving over a period of time. Our team must know this. It allows us to accept loss as an indication of the improvements we must make. In this sense there are no "winners" in the world and there are no "losers." As we improve our skills, we become more winner-like than we are loser-like. Winning is not some anointed place that one achieves.

The winner-like team makes a total commitment to trying to win. It does not go in tentatively or hopefully or naively. It combines great talent and a love for the game with an intense effort and desire. And it has the courage to accept losses in ways that teach it how to be the best.

## Summary

To make it happen, you must first build the engine. This requires total involvement on your part. You have to communicate your vision *and* model it at the same time that you are trying to work on every aspect of your organization.

Fortunately, you do not have to keep this up forever, because it would kill you if you did. The right executive team will help you transition to a less-involved phase. Throughout both phases, your aim is to build a devotion to the ethic of the game—to always improving. Everything you do seeks to create an environment that demands performance and creates the desire to win.

# Notes

**INTRODUCTION**

1. "Lame Duck," *Los Angeles Times.*
2. University of Oregon Sports Information.
3. *1994 USC Football Media Guide*, p. 31, *1995 USC Football Media Guide*, p. 113, University of Southern California, Sports Information Center, Los Angeles, CA.
4. Bettmann Archives.

**CHAPTER 1**

1. "USC Bowl Game Summaries," p. 142, *1995 USC Football Media Guide.*
2. "USC Bowl Game Summaries," p. 147, *1995 USC Football Media Guide.*
3. "College football loses if Pac-10 cuts its ties with the Rose Bowl," *San Diego Union-Tribune*, 6/24/95.
4. "John's Pledge," *Sports*, September 1993.
5. Arthur B. VanGundy, *Brain Boosters for Business Advantage*, Pfeiffer & Company, San Diego, 1995.

**CHAPTER 2**

1. John Gardner, *Self-Renewal*, W.W. Norton & Co., New York, 1981.
2. "Robinson on Walsh, too much pride, too little fun," *San Diego Union-Tribune*, 11/30/94.
3. "Work and Family," *The Wall Street Journal*, 6/14/95.
4. *1994 USC Football Media Guide*, p. 14.

**CHAPTER 4**

1. Thomas J. Peters and Robert H. Waterman, Jr., *In Search of Excellence*, Harper Collins, New York, 1982.

**CHAPTER 5**

1. *1995 USC Football Media Guide*, p. 248, University of Southern California Sports Information Center, Los Angeles, CA.

# Index

## PRAISE FOR JOHN ROBINSON

*"John Robinson is one of the most respected coaches
in the country. He is known to be a great motivator
and a great recruiter. He is also known to be a great teacher
who has inspired many young athletes to outstanding
careers. I am deeply impressed by his commitment."*

Steven Sample
President, USC


*"John Robinson was the single most important person
I ever met. He was the person who let me know how good
I could be. I needed to try some things on my own
to find out what kind of football player I was
and Robinson encouraged me to do that."*

Ahmad Rashad, NBC Sports Commentator
St. Louis Cardinals 1972-73, Buffalo Bills 1973-75, Seattle
Seahawks 1975-76, Minnesota Vikings 1976-82


*"You know what he [Robinson] knows,
so you give him a lot of respect."*

Rob Johnson, All-American quarterback, USC
Jacksonville Jaguars 1995


*"John Robinson is a master recruiter, maybe the best there
is...when [he] returned to USC, talk was that you couldn't
recruit there anymore. This year, he's brought in too many
prep and JC All-Americans to count. This year's class is
regarded in some circles as the country's best."*

Nick Canepa, *San Diego Union Tribune*


*"Robinson preaches power."*

*Daily News*

*"He doesn't hesitate to use authority.*
*But he doesn't run over people to do it."*

R.C. Slocum
Head Coach, Texas A&M

*"He's a very organized guy. He knows exactly what*
*he wants to do...but he's also very flexible.*
*He won't hesitate to change things around if he has to.*
*He has a way of making the staff meetings very productive,*
*yet also a lot of fun."*

Mike Sanford
USC Assistant Coach, Wide Receivers

*"Robinson has a history of being wonderfully candid...he*
*always left you with something rich and crunchy*
*and delightfully quotable that your readers*
*could chew on all week."*

Phil Elderkin
*Southern California Magazine*

*"He [Robinson] was always coming into my office*
*with some play he'd drawn up—he'd say 'Coach,*
*we gotta try this one'...Yes, I could see he'd be a coach.*
*He was brimming with ideas."*

Len Casanova
Former Head Coach, University of Oregon

*"John Robinson may be on the verge of something big."*

*Street and Smith's College Football '95*

# THE WARREN BENNIS EXECUTIVE BRIEFING SERIES

*"To survive in the 21st century, we're going to need
a new generation of leaders, not managers.
This series is an exciting collection of business books
written to help your leaders meet the challenges of the new millennium."*

Dr. Warren Bennis
USC Professor and Founding Chairman, The Leadership Institute
Author, *On Becoming a Leader* and *An Invented Life*

Tailored to the needs of busy professionals and authored by subject matter experts, the *Warren Bennis Executive Briefing Series* helps leaders acquire significant knowledge in the face of information overload. All *Series* titles utilize the SuperReading comprehension/retention editing and design techniques made famous by Howard Berg, *The Guinness Book of World Records'* "World's Fastest Reader." Read these 128-page books in just two hours!

## TITLES INCLUDE:

| | |
|---|---|
| *Fabled Service: Ordinary Acts, Extraordinary Outcome* | Betsy Sanders |
| *The 21st Century Organization:*<br>  *Reinventing Through Reengineering* | Warren Bennis/<br>Michael Mische |
| *Managing Globalization in the Age of Interdependence* | George Lodge |
| *Coach to Coach: Business Lessons from the Locker Room* | John Robinson |
| *The Faster Learning Organization:*<br>  *Gain and Sustain the Competitive Edge* | Bob Guns |
| *The Absolutes of Leadership* | Philip Crosby |
| *Customer Inspired Quality:*<br>  *Looking Backward Through the Telescope* | James Shaw |
| *INFORelief: Stay Afloat in the InfoFlood* | Maureen Malunchuk |

Contact your local bookstore for all *Warren Bennis Executive Briefing Series* titles, or order directly from Pfeiffer & Company Customer Service, **1-800-274-4434**, 2780 Circleport Drive, Erlanger, KY, 41018. For Special Sales or bulk purchases, call Pfeiffer & Company Group Sales at 1-800-320-2270.